Everywoman's Diet Handbook

Everywoman's Diet Handbook

COMPILED AND EDITED BY

Carol Tiffany

NELSON DOUBLEDAY, INC.
Garden City, New York

Contents

Introduction *1*
Eat Well, Keep Well *3*
Height/Weight Chart *9*
Daily Maintenance Calorie Chart *10*
Food & Drink Counter *11*
Low-Calorie Menus *54*
Low-Calorie Recipes *61*
  Appetizers
  Soups
  Meats
  Poultry and Seafood
  Vegetables
  Salads and Salad Dressings
  Desserts
Calorie Counter/Calories Burned Per Hour *93*
Vitamin Counter *96*

Introduction

Here, at last, is a compact compendium of everything you need to know about diet and nutrition. In this easy-to-use handbook, you'll find all the facts at your fingertips on how to

- Eat Slim/Keep Trim
- Count your Calories/Count your Carbohydrates (or Fats or Proteins or Vitamins)
- Chart your way to Total Nutrition

So you want to be healthy/healthier? Looking good, feeling just right? With the help of this comprehensive collection of nutritional tools, you can make *today* Day One of a healthier, happier, more natural self.

Are you always trying to lose "just five more pounds"? Don't despair. Eating right and eating *light* can be enjoyable if you know how to eat well, if you know what you are eating and why.

The Doubleday Cookbook, extensively researched and written by Jean Anderson and Elaine Hanna, supplies a host of low-calorie recipes—simple and delicious recipes with just a bit of a difference, whether it be an appetizer spread made out of eggplant, a meat loaf with rolled oats, or an apple soup.

You'll also find a week's menus for a 1200-calorie-a-day diet, each menu delightfully varied and perfectly balanced, as well as interesting background material on the essential nutrients and on the four basic food groups—all from *The Doubleday Cookbook.*

Perhaps you are more concerned with counting carbohydrates (or fats or proteins) than counting calories. The *Food & Drink Counter* gives information on all of them (calories, too) in its listing of over 1000 items.

Or perhaps your weight is under control, but you are smart enough to want to balance your nutrients, and to keep an eye on your vitamin intake. In that case, just turn to the *Vitamin Counter* at the back where you'll find over 1000 foods and beverages listed, along with a detailed rundown on each of the major vitamins.

1

Have you discovered that the only way you can maintain your weight is by expending extra calories through exercise? The *Calorie Counter/Calories Burned Per Hour* is a unique table that will show you just how many calories are used up during an hour's worth of over 30 daily activities and sports. At 1222 calories burned per hour for a 125-pound woman, don't you think you might want to start running in place (at the rate of 140 counts a minute)? If that's too strenuous, there's always square dancing or tennis at around 350 calories per hour (while eating and sleeping are only 60 to 70 calories per hour). Take your pick; there's no excuse now that you know the facts.

What should you weigh, ideally? How many calories should you consume to maintain that weight? What exactly is in that tasty turnip, that sinful sundae? Just turn to the appropriate chart or counter. Everything is here in this handy, quick-reference book, a complete handbook that you'll find indispensable.

Look forward to looking good, feeling good—by eating right.

CAROL TIFFANY

2

Eat Well, Keep Well

Astonishing as it may seem in this age of abundance, a great many Americans are malnourished. Not for lack of money. But for lack of understanding about how foods function in the body. We tend to eat what we like, often without restraint, and in America preferences run to carbohydrates (starches and sweets).

What we eat affects how we look, feel, and to some extent behave. The killing and crippling diseases of yesterday—scurvy, pellagra, beriberi, rickets—were all eventually traced to specific nutritional deficiencies, a vitamin C deficiency for scurvy, niacin for pellagra, thiamine for beriberi, and vitamin D for rickets. Such desperate vitamin inadequacies, fortunately, are rarely seen in America today, but poor nutrition manifests itself in bad complexions and other skin problems, in obesity, in irritability and listlessness.

Nutritionists maintain that, with rare exceptions, a person who eats moderately and wisely, selecting a variety of foods each day from The 4 Basic Food Groups, will be properly nourished.

THE 4 BASIC FOOD GROUPS

GROUP I—THE MILK GROUP: Milk (all kinds), cream, cheese needed to supply calcium, high-quality protein, vitamin A, and riboflavin (a B vitamin). The *Recommended Daily Amount* varies according to age and sex:

	8-ounce glasses needed per day
Children under 9	2–3
Children 9–12	3 or more
Teen-agers	4 or more
Adults	2 or more
Pregnant Women	3 or more
Nursing Mothers	4 or more

Note: Some "milk" may be taken as cheese or ice cream:

½ cup ice cream=¼ cup milk
½ cup cottage cheese=⅓ cup milk
1 (1″) cube Cheddar cheese=½ cup milk

GROUP II—THE MEAT GROUP: All meats and organ meats, poultry and eggs, fish and shellfish, and, as occasional meat substitutes, dry beans and peas, lentils, nuts, and peanut butter. This group supplies the body with top quality protein, iron, and three important B vitamins—thiamine, riboflavin, and niacin. *Recommended Daily Amounts:* 2 or more servings from the group. Any of the following count as 1 serving: 3 ounces cooked lean meat, poultry or seafood; 2 eggs; 1 cup cooked dried beans, peas or lentils; ¼ cup peanut butter.

GROUP III—THE FRUIT AND VEGETABLE GROUP: The source of vitamin-A-rich foods (dark green and yellow vegetables such as broccoli and winter squash and such fruits as apricots, cantaloupe, mangoes, persimmons, and pumpkin); also the source of vitamin-C-rich foods (citrus fruits, cantaloupe, strawberries, sweet green and red peppers). *Recommended Amounts:* 1 serving daily of a vitamin-C-rich food, 1 serving every other day of a vitamin A food, and 2–3 additional servings daily of any other foods in the group.

GROUP IV—THE BREAD-CEREAL GROUP: All whole grains, enriched or restored breads and cereals, necessary for B vitamins, protein, iron, and energy. *Recommended Daily Amounts:* 4 or more servings, 5 or more if breads only are eaten.

OTHER FOODS: Fats, oils, sweets, refined cereals are all important to the body as energy foods. But they are so rarely lacking in the diet it's not necessary to remind people to eat them.

ABOUT INDIVIDUAL NUTRIENTS

What are proteins exactly? Carbohydrates? Vitamins? Minerals? What do they do in the body? Why are they important?

Protein: The substance of life, the body's building material. It is essential to the maintenance and repair of all bodily tissues, to the production of enzymes, hormones, and infection-fighting antibodies. Protein also provides energy to fuel the body. In truth, protein is not a single compound but many, composed of simpler compounds called *amino acids.* To date, 22 amino acids have been isolated, eight of them *essential,* meaning the body cannot manufacture them and that they must be taken in as food. The highest quality proteins are those providing the best supply of essential amino acids—animal foods, invariably, such as meat, seafood, poultry, milk, cheese, and eggs.

Carbohydrates: The sugars and starches, the body's main sources of energy. Some carbohydrates are immediately absorbed into the bloodstream, providing instant energy, while others are stored for future use. Adequate amounts of complex, unrefined carbohydrates allow the body to save proteins for use in body building and repair. Indigestible carbohydrates are known as dietary fiber (roughage). Fiber is not a nutrient, but it is essential to the healthy functioning of the body, adding bulk, speeding up the digestive process, and stimulating elimination. Carbohydrates are found in grains, vegetables, legumes and fruits.

Fats and Oils: Complex chemical substances, controversial today because they have been implicated in circulatory and heart diseases. Their chief role in the body is to provide energy, and this they do, about twice as well as carbohydrates and proteins. But the specter of *cholesterol* looms and television commercials, hammering away at us to use this mono- or polyunsaturated fat, won't let us forget it. Cholesterol is not a fat but a related fatty substance used by the body to form vitamin D and certain hormones. Its presence in the body (particularly its accumulation in and clogging of blood vessels) is being investigated in relation to the saturation of a fat. Saturation refers, simply, to the hydrogen content of a fat and, in a far more practical sense, to the consistency. Generally speaking, the more hydrogen a fat contains, the more saturated it is and the harder or stiffer.

Vitamins: These chemical compounds, found in minute quantities in foods, are essential to good health. The most important of them are:

Vitamin A: Helps eyes adjust to changing light intensities, helps prevent night blindness, necessary for healthy mucous membranes. *Good Sources:* Dark yellow or orange fruits, dark green and yellow vegetables, cream, butter, whole milk, fortified margarine, liver. (*Note:* Vitamin A can be stored by the body, so avoid overdoses of vitamin pills.)

5

The B Group: There are about a dozen B vitamins, the most important of which are *thiamine* (B_1), *riboflavin* (B_2), and *niacin.* If the body receives enough of these three, it is unlikely to be deficient in any others of the B group.

Thiamine helps keep muscles, heart, and nerves functioning properly, promotes appetite and aids carbohydrate metabolism. *Good Sources:* Meat (particularly pork), fish, poultry, enriched breads and cereals, milk, dried peas, and beans.

Riboflavin is essential for the utilization of oxygen within the body and enzyme function. *Good Sources:* The same as for thiamine.

Niacin, like riboflavin, is necessary for proper tissue use of oxygen, also for healthy skin, tongue, and digestive system. *Good Sources:* Lean meats, poultry, whole and enriched cereals, peanuts, dried peas, and beans.

Vitamin C (Ascorbic Acid) has literally to do with holding the body together—tissues, bones, teeth, blood vessels. It speeds healing of wounds, helps stave off infection. *Good Sources:* Citrus fruits, cantaloupe, strawberries, tomatoes, sweet green peppers, raw cabbage, collards and kale, broccoli, freshly dug Irish potatoes.

Vitamin D: Essential to calcium metabolism and the formation of sound bones and teeth. *Good Sources:* Eggs, fish liver oils, sardines, salmon, tuna, sunshine (it converts a substance on the skin to vitamin D which can then be used by the body. *Caution:* Bathing or showering after a sunbath destroys the vitamin D). Like vitamin A, vitamin D can be stored by the body and indiscriminate use of vitamin pills may cause overdoses and illness.

Vitamin E: Despite faddists' cure-all claims for vitamin E, scientists have yet to substantiate any of them. Physicians have used vitamin E successfully to treat a certain anemia in children. Its primary role, however, seems to be as a biological-antioxidant (preventing unwanted oxidation of certain fatty acids) in both the body and in foods. It is important that the diet contain adequate amounts of vitamin E, but because it is so widely found in foods we eat (vegetable oils, eggs, butter and margarine, legumes and nuts, green leafy vegetables, wheat germ), deficiencies are unlikely.

Minerals:

Calcium and Phosphorous: Necessary for strong bones and teeth, good muscle tone, sound nervous system. *Good Sources:* Milk and milk products, dark leafy greens such as kale, collards, mustard and turnip greens.

Iodine: Needed for normal thyroid function. *Good Sources:* Seafood, iodized salt.

Iron: Essential for rich, red blood. *Good Sources:* Organ meats (particularly liver), red meats, oysters, dark green leafy vegetables, eggs, dried fruits, whole or enriched cereals.

Note: There are a number of other minerals and vitamins but they have not been included here either because they are unlikely to be missing in the diet or because their function and requirement are still undetermined.

ABOUT WATER

Though not a nutrient, water is nonetheless vital. The human body, about ⅔ water, must have water in order to survive—to regulate body temperature, to aid digestion, to carry off wastes. Most foods contain water, it's true, but they may not provide the body as much water as it needs. The old rule of "6–8 glasses of liquid a day" still holds.

ABOUT CALORIES

Calories do count, alas, and the only way to lose weight safely and successfully is to reduce the daily calorie intake—forever if necessary. There simply is no magic pill or potion to melt away unwanted pounds. Crash diets do produce immediate results—sometimes drastic ones—but in the long run they fail because the dieter not only regains all lost weight but usually an extra few pounds as well. This sort of seesaw dieting is dangerous. So, too, are starvation diets limiting calories to less than 1000 a day. If you have more than 5 or 10 pounds to lose, see your doctor and have him advise the reducing diet that is

7

best for you. Most doctors discourage losing more than 2–3 pounds a week, and most agree that the only sane way to diet is to eat foods from each of The 4 Basic Food Groups, merely less of each.

What is a calorie? Technically, a unit of heat used to measure the fuel potential of food in the body. To maintain body weight, the calorie intake (via food) must equal the outgo (via energy expended in the day's activities). When the intake exceeds the outgo, the balance is converted to fat. When the reverse is true, as in reducing diets, the body's fat reserves are tapped to provide energy.

"Middle age spread" is simply a failure to adjust eating habits to a slower life-style. We continue to stuff ourselves as we did in our teens and yet are far less active. To compound the problem, our basal metabolism is slowing down. It will continue to decline throughout life, and the woman who would keep her figure will cut daily calorie intake by about 150–200 every 10 years after the age of 25.

The temptation is to watch the scale creep upward, reaching new plateaus, until we realize one day with a start that we are 10 or 20 pounds too heavy. Then come the remorse and the resolutions to diet.

Height/Weight Chart

To thwart the necessity of dieting, consult the following charts which show desirable weights and daily maintenance calories. They'll help you determine at a glance what you should weigh and how to maintain that desired weight:

DESIRABLE WEIGHTS FOR WOMEN, AGE 25 AND OVER*
Note: for girls between 18 and 25, subtract 1 pound for each year under 25.

Height (in shoes, 2″ heels)		*Weight in Pounds* (*in indoor clothing*)		
		Small Frame	Medium Frame	Large Frame
Feet	Inches			
4	10	92–98	96–107	104–119
4	11	94–101	98–110	106–122
5	0	96–104	101–113	109–125
5	1	99–107	104–116	112–128
5	2	102–110	107–119	115–131
5	3	105–113	110–122	118–134
5	4	108–116	113–126	121–138
5	5	111–119	116–130	125–142
5	6	114–123	120–135	129–146
5	7	118–127	124–139	133–150
5	8	122–131	128–143	137–154
5	9	126–135	132–147	141–158
5	10	130–140	136–151	145–163
5	11	134–144	140–155	149–168
6	0	138–148	144–159	153–173

* Prepared by the Metropolitan Life Insurance Company.

Daily Maintenance Calorie Chart

DAILY MAINTENANCE CALORIES*

	desired weight	18–35 years	35–55 years	55–75 years
	99	1,700	1,500	1,300
	110	1,850	1,650	1,400
	121	2,000	1,750	1,550
	128	2,100	1,900	1,600
WOMEN	132	2,150	1,950	1,650
	143	2,300	2,050	1,800
	154	2,400	2,150	1,850
	165	2,550	2,300	1,950

* Based on moderate activity. If your life is very active, add calories; if you lead a sedentary life, subtract calories.

Food & Drink Counter

Now that you know how many calories you can safely consume in a day, all you need to do is keep track of your caloric intake. It's easy with the Food & Drink Counter which lists calories for over 1000 foods and beverages. And if you are interested in the carbohydrate, protein and fat contents, these are listed as well.

HOW TO USE THE COUNTER

Are strawberries higher in carbohydrates than blueberries? Does tomato juice have more calories than orange juice? Which is fattier, a pork chop or a lamb chop? Does cottage cheese really contain lots of protein? The answers to these (and many more) questions are easily found in the Counter. Here, you'll discover over 1000 foods and beverages listed alphabetically along with their calorie, protein, fat and carbohydrate content—a bible for dieters!

Whether you're watching calories or carbohydrates, the Counter is indispensable for meal-planning. Just flip to the foods in question to see if they fit in with the daily allowance of your diet. If not, it's easy to find substitutes. If you're slimming the high-protein way, the Counter gives protein gram counts for quick tallying and identifies protein-high menu items. For those who must limit their fat intake, the listing of each food's fat content automatically pinpoints foods which are permitted, and those which are not. And even if you're not dieting, the Counter will help you to plan family meals based on principles of sound nutrition.

Note that foods listed are specific. For example, you will find a listing for canned tuna, but not for tuna salad. Why? Because your tuna salad may be made with pickles and two dollops of mayonnaise while your mother may use diced celery and one tablespoon of mayo. Differences of this sort make accuracy impossible. What we've done is to list basic foods only. To calculate the precise number of calories —or carbohydrate grams, etc.—in your *own* tuna salad, simply look up each ingredient you use, then total the amounts.

Weights and Measures

Whenever possible, foods are given in common household measures (e.g., 1 cup, 4 ounces, 1 tablespoon, etc.). If you want to be truly accurate, pay close attention to the gram weights listed—they're indisputably correct. An inexpensive gram scale is a good investment, especially helpful in determining foods listed by size. Say you want to eat a Florida orange. It's listed this way:

". . . 1 average (3" diameter) . . ."

The gram weight listing is 210 grams. To avoid measuring fruit with a tapemeasure, simply estimate its size when buying in the supermarket, and when you get home, weigh it. If it's only 190 grams, it's about 10% smaller than the orange listed. Adjust all food values downward by 10%.

All portions specified in the Counter pertain only to the edible part of the food. How is this important? It's not if you're drinking a glass of milk which is 100% edible. But if you're eating watermelon, bear this in mind: an entire wedge of juicy melon may weigh about two pounds and that number will be the gram weight indicated. However, the food value applies only to that part of the watermelon that's edible—which is approximately 25% of the entire wedge. Or, if you're having an 8-ounce T-bone steak and 50% of it is bone, the food values shown apply for only four ounces of steak.

Food Preparation

Naturally, food values will change depending on how food is prepared. Check the Counter to see what preparation, if any, is specified. Whenever you see the word "prepared" (or "prepared with milk") as part of a listing, it means that all figures apply to the food, ready to be eaten, prepared with listed ingredients. If you plan to deviate from those ingredients—for example, by substituting skim milk for whole—adjust food values accordingly.

Abbreviations:

oz.	ounce
lb.	pound
gm.	gram
n.a.	not available (lack of reliable data)
tr.	trace

12

FOOD AND MEASURE	Weight (gm.)	Calories	Protein (gm.)	Fat (gm.)	Carbo- hydrate (gm.)
Abalone, canned, 4 oz.	114	91	18.1	.3	2.6
Acerola juice, 6-oz. glass	188	43	.8	.6	9.0
Alcoholic beverages:					
beer, 4.5% alcohol, 12-oz. glass	360	151	n.a.	n.a.	13.7
pure distilled gin, rum, whiskey, vodka, etc.:					
80-proof, 1½-oz. jigger	42	97	n.a.	n.a.	tr.
90-proof, 1½-oz. jigger	42	110	n.a.	n.a.	tr.
100-proof, 1½-oz. jigger	42	124	n.a.	n.a.	tr.
wine, dessert, 18.8% alcohol, 3½-oz. glass	103	141	.1	0	7.9
wine, table, 12.2% alcohol, 3½-oz. glass	102	87	.1	0	4.3
Almonds, dried, in shell, 4 oz.	114	346	10.8	31.4	11.3
dried, shelled, 4 oz.	114	678	21.1	61.5	22.1
dried, shelled, ½ cup	71	425	13.2	38.5	13.8
roasted, shelled, 4 oz.	114	711	21.1	65.4	22.1
roasted, shelled, ½ cup	78	489	14.5	45.0	15.2
chopped, ½ cup	64	401	11.9	36.9	12.5
candy and chocolate-coated, see Candies					
Anchovies, canned in oil, 1 oz.	28	50	5.4	2.9	tr.
Anchovy paste, 1 tablespoon	20	42	1.6	2.0	.9
Apple butter, 1 tablespoon	15	28	tr.	.1	7.0
Apple juice, canned, 6-oz. glass	187	91	.2	tr.	22.2
Apples, raw, average variety, whole, 1 lb.	454	242	.8	2.5	60.5
raw, unpared, 1 average (about 3 per lb.)	150	80	.3	.8	20.0
raw, pared, diced, 1 cup	109	59	.2	.3	15.4
dried, cooked, sweetened, 1 cup	280	314	.8	1.0	81.5
dried, cooked, unsweetened, 1 cup	260	202	.8	1.2	52.5
frozen, sweetened, 4 oz.	114	105	.2	.1	27.5
Applesauce, canned, sweetened, 1 cup	255	232	.5	.3	60.7
Applesauce, canned, unsweetened, 1 cup	244	100	.5	.5	26.3
Apricot nectar, canned, 6-oz. glass	188	107	.6	.2	27.4

13

FOOD AND MEASURE	Weight (gm.)	Calories	Protein (gm.)	Fat (gm.)	Carbohydrate (gm.)
Apricots, raw, whole, 1 lb.	454	217	4.3	.9	54.6
raw, 1 average (about 12 per lb.)	38	18	.4	tr.	4.5
raw, pitted, halved, 1 cup	156	80	1.6	.3	19.9
canned in heavy syrup, 1 cup	252	217	1.5	.2	55.4
dried, uncooked, 1 cup	150	390	7.5	.7	99.7
dried, cooked, sweetened, 1 cup	325	396	4.6	.3	102.2
dried, cooked, unsweetened, 1 cup	285	242	4.6	.6	61.6
frozen, sweetened, 1 cup	260	256	1.8	.2	65.2
candied, 1 oz.	28	96	.1	tr.	24.5
Artichoke hearts, frozen, 3 average	85	22	1.2	.2	4.9
Artichokes, French, boiled, 1 average	120	53	3.3	.3	11.9
Asparagus, raw spears, 1 lb.	454	66	6.4	.5	12.7
fresh, cooked, drained, 4 spears	60	12	1.3	.1	2.2
fresh cuts, cooked, drained, 1 cup	145	29	3.2	.3	5.2
canned spears, drained, 1 cup	215	45	5.2	.9	7.3
frozen spears, 4 oz.	114	27	3.6	.2	4.4
frozen cuts and tips, 1 cup	180	41	5.9	.4	6.5
Avocados, California, peeled, pitted, ½ average	108	185	2.4	18.3	6.5
Florida, peeled, pitted, ½ average	123	157	1.6	13.5	10.8
diced, 1 cup	147	245	3.1	24.1	9.3
mashed, 1 cup	231	386	4.8	37.9	14.5

B

FOOD AND MEASURE	Weight (gm.)	Calories	Protein (gm.)	Fat (gm.)	Carbohydrate (gm.)
Bacon, cooked crisp, drained, 2 slices	15	92	4.5	7.8	.5
Bacon, Canadian, cooked crisp, drained, 1 slice	15	42	4.1	2.6	tr.
Bagel, water, 1 medium (3″ diameter)	55	165	6.0	2.0	30.0
Bamboo shoots, fresh, 4 oz.	114	31	2.9	.3	5.9
Bananas, peeled, 1 medium	119	101	1.3	.2	26.4
sliced, 1 cup	146	124	1.6	.3	32.4

14

baking type, plantain, peeled, 1 medium	126	150	1.4	.5	39.3
Barbecue sauce, 1 cup	250	228	3.7	17.2	20.0
Barley, pearled, light, uncooked, 1 cup	200	698	16.4	2.0	157.6
Bass, sea, raw, 4 oz.	114	116	21.9	1.4	0
Bass, striped, raw, 4 oz.	114	120	21.5	3.1	0
Bean sprouts, mung, raw, 1 cup	90	32	3.4	.2	6.0
Bean sprouts, soy, raw, 1 cup	107	49	6.6	1.5	5.7
Baked beans, canned, in tomato sauce, 8 oz.	227	272	14.3	1.1	52.2
with frankfurters, 8 oz.	227	327	17.3	16.1	28.6
with pork in tomato sauce, 8 oz.	227	277	13.8	5.9	43.1
with pork in molasses sauce, 8 oz.	227	340	14.0	10.7	47.8
Beans, green or snap, raw, whole, 1 lb.	454	128	7.6	.8	28.3
fresh, boiled, drained, cuts, 1 cup	130	33	2.1	.3	7.0
canned, cuts, drained, 1 cup	140	34	2.0	.3	7.3
frozen, cuts, boiled, drained, 1 cup	160	40	2.5	.2	9.1
Beans, lima, raw, immature, in pods, 1 lb.	454	223	15.2	.9	40.1
fresh, boiled, drained, 1 cup	170	189	12.9	.9	33.7
canned, drained, 1 cup	175	168	9.5	.5	32.0
frozen, baby, boiled, drained, 1 cup	173	204	12.8	.3	38.6
frozen, fordhook, boiled, drained, 1 cup	168	166	10.1	.2	32.1
Beans, red kidney, dry, 1 cup	186	638	41.8	2.8	115.1
cooked, drained, 1 cup	185	218	14.4	.9	39.6
canned, with liquid, 1 cup	256	230	14.6	1.0	41.9
Beans, wax, fresh, boiled, drained, 1 cup	140	31	2.0	.3	6.4
Beans, wax, canned, drained, 1 cup	140	34	1.6	.4	7.3
Beans, white, boiled, drained, 1 cup	190	224	14.8	1.1	40.3
Beechnuts, shelled, 4 oz.	114	644	22.0	56.7	23.0
Beef, choice grade, retail trim, meat only, 4 oz.: chuck, boneless arm, pot roasted, lean and fat	114	329	30.9	21.8	0

15

FOOD AND MEASURE	Weight (gm.)	Calories	Protein (gm.)	Fat (gm.)	Carbo-hydrate (gm.)
chuck, boneless arm, pot roasted, lean only	114	220	34.7	7.9	0
club steak, broiled, lean and fat	114	517	23.5	46.3	0
club steak, broiled, lean only	114	278	33.7	14.8	0
flank steak, pot roasted	114	223	34.8	8.3	0
ground, regular, broiled	114	326	27.6	23.1	0
ground, lean, broiled	114	250	31.2	12.9	0
porterhouse steak, broiled, lean and fat	114	530	22.4	48.1	0
porterhouse steak, broiled, lean only	114	255	34.4	11.9	0
rib, roasted, lean and fat	114	502	22.7	44.9	0
rib, roasted, lean only	114	275	32.1	15.2	0
round, broiled, lean and fat	114	297	32.6	17.5	0
round, broiled, lean only	114	214	35.5	6.9	0
rump, roasted, lean and fat	114	395	26.9	31.1	0
rump, roasted, lean only	114	237	33.1	10.6	0
sirloin steak, double-bone, broiled, lean and fat	114	465	25.3	39.5	0
sirloin steak, double-bone, broiled, lean only	114	246	34.8	10.8	0
sirloin steak, round-bone, broiled, lean and fat	114	441	26.2	36.5	0
sirloin steak, round-bone, broiled, lean only	114	236	36.7	8.7	0
T-bone steak, broiled, lean and fat	114	539	22.2	49.2	0
T-bone steak, lean only	114	254	34.6	11.7	0
Beef, corned, boiled, medium fat, 4 oz.	114	424	26.1	34.6	0
canned, medium fat, 4 oz.	114	245	28.7	13.6	0
canned, lean, 4 oz.	114	210	29.9	9.1	0
canned, hash, with potato, 1 cup	220	398	19.4	24.9	23.5
Beef, dried or chipped, uncooked, 4 oz.	114	231	39.1	6.2	0
Beef liver, see Liver					
Beef pot pie, frozen, 8-oz. pie	227	436	16.6	22.5	40.9
Beef, potted, 4 oz.	114	283	19.9	21.9	0
Beef, roast, canned, 4 oz.	114	254	28.3	14.8	0

16

Food					
Beef stew, with vegetables, canned, 8 oz.	227	179	13.2	7.0	16.1
Beef tongue, see Tongue					
Beer, see Alcoholic Beverages					
Beet greens, boiled, drained, 1 cup	200	36	3.4	.4	6.6
Beets, raw, 1 medium (2″ diameter)	50	21	.8	tr.	4.9
fresh, diced, boiled, drained, 1 cup	180	58	2.0	.2	12.9
fresh, sliced, boiled, drained, 1 cup	205	66	2.2	.2	14.8
canned, diced, drained, 1 cup	163	60	1.6	.2	14.3
canned, sliced, drained, 1 cup	176	65	1.8	.2	15.5
Biscuit dough, canned, chilled, 4 oz.	114	318	8.3	7.3	52.9
Biscuit mix, baked with milk, 1-oz. biscuit	28	92	2.0	2.6	14.8
Blackberries, fresh, 1 cup	146	85	1.8	1.3	18.8
canned, with heavy syrup, 1 cup	260	237	2.1	1.6	57.7
frozen, sweetened, 1 cup	252	242	2.0	.8	61.5
Blueberries, fresh, 1 cup	146	90	1.2	.4	35.6
canned, with heavy syrup, 1 cup	250	253	1.0	.5	65.0
frozen, sweetened, 1 cup	228	239	1.4	.7	60.4
frozen, unsweetened, 1 cup	165	91	1.2	.8	22.4
Bluefish, baked or broiled with butter, 4 oz.	114	181	29.9	5.9	0
Bockwurst, 4 oz.	114	301	12.9	27.0	.7
Bologna, all meat, 4 oz.	114	312	14.9	25.6	4.2
Bologna, with cereal added, 4 oz.	114	299	16.2	23.5	4.4
Bouillon cube, ½″ cube	4	5	.8	.1	.2
Brains, all kinds, raw, 4 oz.	114	142	11.8	9.8	.9
Braunschweiger, 4 oz.	114	364	16.9	31.2	2.6
Brazil nuts, shelled, 4 oz.	114	741	16.2	75.9	12.4
shelled, 1 cup	142	929	20.3	95.0	15.5
shelled, 2–3 nuts	10	65	1.4	6.7	1.1
Bread, Boston brown, 1 slice, 3″ × ¾″	48	101	2.6	.6	21.9
cracked wheat, 1 slice (20 per loaf)	23	60	2.0	.5	11.9
French or Vienna, 1 slice, 3¼″ × 2″ × 1″	20	58	1.8	.6	11.1
Italian, 1 slice, 3¼″ × 2″ × 1″	20	55	1.8	.1	11.3

FOOD AND MEASURE	Weight (gm.)	Calories	Protein (gm.)	Fat (gm.)	Carbo-hydrate (gm.)
pumpernickel, 1 slice,					
3¾" × 3¾" × ⅛"	30	74	2.7	.4	15.9
raisin, 1 slice (20 per loaf)	23	60	1.5	.6	12.3
rye, light, 1 slice (20 per loaf)	23	56	2.1	.2	11.9
white, 1 slice (20 per loaf)	23	62	2.0	.7	11.6
white, 1 thin slice (26 per loaf)	17	46	1.5	.5	8.6
whole wheat, 1 slice					
(20 per loaf)	23	56	2.4	.7	11.0
Breadcrumbs, dry, grated, 1 cup	102	400	12.9	4.7	74.9
Bread sticks, Vienna, 1 oz.	28	86	2.7	.9	16.4
Bread sticks, regular, 1 oz.	28	109	3.4	.8	21.3
Bread stuffing mix, dry, 1 cup	71	263	9.1	2.7	51.4
Breadfruit, peeled and trimmed,					
4 oz.	114	117	1.0	.3	29.9
Broccoli, raw, trimmed spears,					
1 lb.	454	89	10.0	.8	16.3
fresh, spears, boiled, drained,					
1 cup	150	39	4.6	.4	6.7
fresh, cuts, boiled, drained,					
1 cup	155	40	4.8	.5	7.0
frozen, spears, 10-oz. package	283	79	9.3	.6	14.4
frozen, chopped, boiled,					
drained, 1 cup	188	49	5.5	.6	8.6
Brussels sprouts, fresh, boiled,					
drained, 1 cup	180	65	7.6	.7	11.5
Brussels sprouts, frozen, boiled,					
drained, 1 cup	188	62	6.0	.4	12.2
Bulgar, parboiled wheat, club,					
dry, 4 oz.	114	407	9.7	1.6	90.2
hard red winter, dry, 4 oz.	114	401	12.7	1.7	85.8
white, dry, 4 oz.	114	405	11.7	1.4	88.6
canned, hard red winter,					
seasoned, 1 cup	135	246	8.4	4.5	44.3
Butter, 1 cup or ½ lb.	227	1625	1.4	183.9	.9
1 tablespoon	14	100	.1	11.3	tr.
whipped, 1 stick or ½ cup	76	544	.5	61.5	.3
whipped, 1 tablespoon	9	64	.1	7.3	tr.
Butter oil, 1 tablespoon	14	123	tr.	13.9	0
Buttermilk, see Milk					
Butternuts, shelled, 4 oz.	114	713	26.9	69.4	9.5
Butternuts, 4–5 nuts	15	94	3.5	9.2	1.3

Cabbage, common, raw, trimmed, 1 lb.	454	98	5.3	.8	22.0
common, raw, chopped, 1 cup	89	21	1.2	.2	4.8
common, raw, coarse shredded, 1 cup	70	22	.9	.1	3.8
common, shredded, boiled, drained, 1 cup	145	29	1.6	.3	6.2
common, raw, salad, see Coleslaw					
red, raw, trimmed, 1 lb.	454	127	8.2	.8	28.2
red, raw, coarse shredded, 1 cup	70	22	1.4	.1	4.8
savoy, raw, trimmed, 1 lb.	454	98	9.8	.8	18.8
savoy, raw, coarse shredded, 1 cup	70	17	1.7	.1	3.2
Cabbage, Chinese, raw, 1" cuts, 1 cup	75	11	.9	.1	2.2
Cabbage, Chinese, raw, strips, 1 cup	59	8	.7	.1	1.8
Cabbage, spoon, raw, 1 lb.	454	69	6.9	.9	12.5
Cabbage, spoon, boiled, drained, 1 cup	170	24	2.4	.3	4.1
Cake mixes, prepared, 4-oz. piece:					
angel food, prepared with water, flavoring	114	295	6.5	.2	67.7
chocolate malt, prepared with eggs, water, icing	114	394	3.9	9.9	75.9
coffeecake, prepared with eggs, milk	114	367	7.2	10.9	59.7
devil's food, prepared with eggs, water, icing	114	386	5.0	14.0	66.5
gingerbread, prepared with water	114	315	3.5	7.8	58.2
honey spice, prepared with eggs, water, icing	114	401	4.8	12.3	69.4
marble, prepared with eggs, water, icing	114	377	5.0	9.9	70.7
white, prepared with egg whites, water, icing	114	400	4.4	12.2	71.6
yellow, prepared with eggs, water, icing	114	384	4.7	12.9	65.7
Cake, devil's food, frozen, with icing, 4 oz.	114	433	4.9	20.1	63.4

FOOD AND MEASURE	Weight (gm.)	Calories	Protein (gm.)	Fat (gm.)	Carbo-hydrate (gm.)
Candies, 1 oz.:					
almonds, chocolate coated	28	161	3.5	12.4	11.2
almonds, sugar coated	28	129	2.2	5.3	19.9
butterscotch	28	112	tr.	1.0	26.9
candy corn	28	103	tr.	.6	25.4
caramel, plain or chocolate	28	113	1.1	2.9	21.7
caramel, plain or chocolate, with nuts	28	121	1.3	4.6	20.0
caramel, chocolate flavored roll	28	112	.6	2.3	23.4
chocolate, bittersweet	28	135	2.2	11.2	13.2
chocolate, milk	28	147	2.2	9.2	16.1
chocolate, milk, with almonds	28	151	2.6	10.1	14.5
chocolate, milk, with peanuts	28	154	4.0	10.8	12.6
chocolate, milk, sugar coated	28	132	1.5	5.6	20.6
chocolate, semi-sweet	28	144	1.2	10.1	16.2
chocolate, sweet	28	147	1.2	9.9	16.4
chocolate fudge, chocolate coated	28	122	1.1	4.5	20.7
chocolate fudge with nuts, chocolate coated	28	128	1.4	5.9	19.0
coconut, chocolate coated	28	124	.8	5.0	20.4
fondant	28	103	tr.	.6	25.4
fudge, chocolate	28	113	.8	3.5	21.3
fudge, vanilla	28	113	.9	3.1	21.2
fudge, with caramel, nuts, chocolate coated	28	123	2.2	5.1	18.2
fudge, with nuts, caramel, chocolate coated	28	130	2.7	6.5	16.6
hard candy	28	109	0	.3	27.6
jelly beans	28	104	tr.	.1	26.4
marshmallows	28	90	.6	tr.	22.8
mints, uncoated	28	103	tr.	.6	25.4
nougat and caramel, chocolate coated	28	118	1.1	3.9	20.6
peanut brittle	28	119	1.6	2.9	23.0
peanuts, chocolate coated	28	159	4.6	11.7	11.1
raisins, chocolate coated	28	120	1.5	4.8	20.0
Cantaloupe, ½ melon (5" diameter)	385	58	1.4	.2	14.5
Cantaloupe, cubed, 1 cup	162	49	1.1	.2	12.2
Capicola, 4 oz.	114	565	22.9	51.9	0

20

Carrots, raw, 1 medium				
(5½" × 1")	50	21	.5	.1	4.8
raw, grated or shredded, 1 cup	109	46	1.2	.2	10.6
raw, slices, 1 cup	127	53	1.4	.3	12.3
raw, strips, 1 cup	117	49	1.3	.2	11.3
boiled, drained, diced, 1 cup	140	43	1.3	.3	9.9
boiled, drained, slices, 1 cup	153	47	1.4	.3	10.9
canned, diced, drained, 1 cup	159	48	1.3	.5	10.6
Casaba melon, flesh only, 4 oz.	114	31	1.4	tr.	7.4
Casaba melon, cubed, 1 cup	162	44	1.9	tr.	10.5
Cashew nuts, roasted, shelled,					
4 oz.	114	639	19.6	52.1	33.4
Cashew nuts, roasted, shelled,					
1 cup	140	785	24.1	64.0	41.0
Catsup, tomato, bottled,					
1 tablespoon	17	18	.3	tr.	4.3
Cauliflower, raw, flowerets only,					
1 lb.	454	122	12.2	.9	23.6
raw, sliced, 1 cup	83	22	2.2	.2	4.3
boiled, drained, 1 cup	125	28	2.9	.3	5.1
frozen, boiled, drained, 1 cup	179	32	3.4	.4	5.9
Caviar, sturgeon, granular, 1 oz.	28	74	7.6	4.2	1.0
Caviar, sturgeon, pressed, 1 oz.	28	89	9.7	4.7	1.3
Celeriac root, raw, pared, 4 oz.	114	45	2.0	.3	9.6
Celery, raw, 1 outer stalk					
(8" long)	40	7	.4	tr.	1.6
raw, chopped or diced, 1 cup	119	20	1.1	.1	4.6
boiled, drained, diced or					
chunks, 1 cup	153	21	1.2	.2	4.7
boiled, drained, slices, 1 cup	168	24	1.3	.2	5.2
Cereal, ready-to-eat, bran flakes,					
40%, 1 oz.	28	86	2.9	.5	22.8
bran flakes, with raisins, 1 oz.	28	81	2.3	.4	22.5
corn, puffed, presweetened,					
1 oz.	28	107	1.1	tr.	25.4
corn, shredded, 1 oz.	28	110	2.0	.1	24.6
corn flakes, 1 oz.	28	109	2.2	.1	24.2
corn flakes, sugar coated, 1 oz.	28	109	1.2	tr.	25.9
oats, puffed, 1 oz.	28	113	3.4	1.6	21.3
oats, puffed, sugar coated, 1 oz.	28	112	1.9	1.0	24.3
oats, shredded, 1 oz.	28	107	5.3	.6	20.4
rice, puffed, 1 oz.	28	113	1.7	.1	25.4
rice, puffed, presweetened					
with honey, 1 oz.	28	110	1.2	.2	25.7
rice, shredded, 1 oz.	28	111	1.5	.1	25.2

21

FOOD AND MEASURE	Weight (gm.)	Calories	Protein (gm.)	Fat (gm.)	Carbo-hydrate (gm.)
rice flakes, 1 oz.	28	110	1.7	.1	24.9
wheat, puffed, 1 oz.	28	103	4.2	.4	22.3
wheat, puffed, with sugar and honey, 1 oz.	28	107	1.7	.6	25.0
wheat, shredded, 1 oz.	28	100	2.8	.6	22.6
wheat flakes, 1 oz.	28	100	2.9	.4	22.8
wheat germ, toasted, 1 oz.	28	111	8.5	3.2	14.0
Cereal, cooking-type, ¼ cup uncooked:					
farina, enriched	40	148	4.6	.4	30.8
farina, quick cooking	40	145	4.6	.4	30.1
oats, with wheat germ, soy grits	20	76	4.1	1.8	11.7
oatmeal	20	78	2.8	1.5	13.6
wheat, rolled	25	85	2.5	.5	19.1
Cervelat, dry, 4 oz.	114	514	28.0	42.9	1.9
Cervelat, soft, 4 oz.	114	350	21.2	27.9	1.8
Chard, Swiss, raw, trimmed, 1 lb.	454	104	10.0	1.3	19.2
Chard, Swiss, boiled, drained, 1 cup	191	34	3.4	.4	6.3
Cheese, American, processed, 1 oz.	28	105	6.6	8.5	.5
American, processed, shredded, 1 cup	111	411	25.8	33.3	2.1
American, processed, grated, 1 tablespoon	7	28	1.7	2.2	.1
blue or bleu, 1 oz.	28	104	6.1	8.6	.6
brick, 1 oz.	28	105	6.3	8.6	.5
Camembert, 1 oz.	28	85	5.0	7.0	.5
Cheddar, 1 oz.	28	113	7.1	9.1	.6
Cheddar, shredded, 1 cup	111	442	27.8	35.7	2.3
Cheddar, grated, 1 tablespoon	7	28	1.7	2.2	.1
cottage, creamed, 1 oz.	28	30	3.8	1.2	.8
cottage, creamed, 1 cup	245	260	33.3	10.3	7.1
cottage, uncreamed, 1 oz.	28	24	4.8	.1	.8
cottage, uncreamed, 1 cup	200	172	34.0	.6	5.4
cream, 1 oz.	28	106	2.3	10.7	.6
cream, 1 tablespoon	15	56	1.2	5.6	.3
Limburger, 1 oz.	28	98	6.0	7.9	.6
Parmesan, grated, 1 tablespoon	7	28	2.5	1.8	.2
Roquefort, 1 oz.	28	104	6.1	8.6	.6
Swiss, natural, 1 oz.	28	105	7.8	7.9	.5

Swiss, processed, 1 oz.	28	101	7.5	7.6	.5
Cheese food, American, processed, 1 oz.	28	92	5.6	6.8	2.0
Cheese spread, American, processed, 1 oz.	28	82	4.5	6.1	2.3
Cheese straws, 1 oz.	28	128	3.2	8.5	9.8
Cherries, red sour, fresh, with stems, 1 lb.	454	213	4.4	1.1	52.5
red sour, fresh, with pits, 1 cup	160	93	1.9	.5	22.9
red sour, canned in heavy syrup, pitted, 1 cup	235	209	1.9	.5	53.3
red sour, frozen, sweetened, 4 oz.	114	128	1.1	.5	15.3
sweet, fresh, with pits, 1 lb.	454	286	5.3	1.2	71.0
sweet, fresh, with pits, 1 cup	160	112	2.1	.5	27.8
sweet, canned in heavy syrup, pitted, 1 cup	235	190	2.1	.5	48.2
Cherries, candied, 1 oz.	28	96	.1	.1	24.6
Cherries, candied, 1 average	5	17	tr.	tr.	4.3
Cherries, maraschino, bottled, 1 oz.	28	33	.1	.1	8.3
Cherries, maraschino, bottled, 1 average	7	8	tr.	tr.	2.1
Chervil, raw, 4 oz.	114	65	3.9	1.0	13.0
Chestnuts, fresh, shelled, 4 oz.	114	220	3.3	1.7	47.8
Chestnuts, dried, shelled, 4 oz.	114	428	7.6	4.7	89.1
Chewing gum, sweetened, 1 average stick	3	9	n.a.	n.a.	2.8
Chicken, fresh, broiled, meat only, 4 oz.	114	155	27.1	4.3	0
cooked, meat only, diced, 1 cup	134	228	40.2	6.4	0
fried, ½ breast with bone, 3.3 oz.	94	154	24.8	5.0	1.0
fried, drumstick with bone, 2.1 oz.	59	89	11.8	4.0	tr.
roasted, dark meat, 4 oz.	114	210	33.4	7.4	0
roasted, white meat, 4 oz.	114	207	36.8	5.6	0
roasted, meat and skin, 4 oz.	114	283	30.9	16.8	0
stewed, meat only, 4 oz.	114	237	34.2	10.1	0
Chicken, canned, boned, 4 oz.	114	226	24.7	13.3	0
Chicken, potted, 4 oz.	114	283	9.9	21.9	0
Chicken gizzards, boiled, drained, 4 oz.	114	168	30.8	3.8	.8
Chicken liver, see Liver					
Chicken pot pie, frozen, 8-oz. pie	227	497	15.2	26.1	50.4

FOOD AND MEASURE	Weight (gm.)	Calories	Protein (gm.)	Fat (gm.)	Carbo-hydrate (gm.)
Chickpeas, dry, 4 oz.	114	408	23.2	5.4	69.2
Chickpeas, dry, 1 cup	200	720	41.0	9.6	122.0
Chicory greens, untrimmed, 1 lb.	454	74	6.7	1.1	14.1
Chicory greens, 10 inner leaves	25	5	.5	tr.	1.0
Chili con carne, canned, with beans, 8 oz.	227	302	17.0	13.8	27.7
Chili con carne, canned, without beans, 8 oz.	227	454	23.4	33.6	13.2
Chili powder, seasoned, 1 tablespoon	14	52	2.1	1.8	8.1
Chili sauce, tomato, bottled, 1 tablespoon	16	17	.4	tr.	4.0
Chives, raw, 4 oz.	114	32	2.0	.3	6.6
Chocolate, baking-type, bitter, unsweetened, 1 oz.	28	143	3.0	15.0	8.2
semi-sweet, 1 oz.	28	144	1.2	10.1	16.2
semi-sweet, chips or morsels, 1 cup	170	862	7.1	60.7	96.9
sweet, 1 oz.	28	150	1.2	9.9	16.4
Chocolate candy, see Candies					
Chocolate drinks, see Cocoa and Milk					
Chocolate syrup, fudge type, 1 tablespoon	20	66	1.0	2.7	10.8
Chocolate syrup, thin type, 1 tablespoon	20	49	.5	.4	12.5
Chop suey, with meat, canned, 8 oz.	227	141	10.0	7.3	9.5
Chow mein, chicken, canned, 8 oz.	227	86	5.9	.2	16.1
Citron, candied, 1 oz.	28	89	tr.	.1	22.4
Clam juice or liquor, canned, ½ cup	115	22	2.6	.1	2.4
Clams, hard or round, raw, meat only, 8 oz.	227	182	25.2	2.0	13.4
soft, raw, meat only, 8 oz.	227	186	31.8	4.3	3.0
canned, solids and liquid, 4 oz.	114	59	9.0	.8	3.2
canned, drained, 4 oz.	114	112	18.0	2.8	2.2
Cocoa, high fat, processed, 1 tablespoon powder	6	18	1.0	1.4	2.7

medium fat, processed, 1 tablespoon powder	6	16	1.0	1.1	2.9
low medium fat, processed, 1 tablespoon powder	6	13	1.2	.8	3.0
low fat, 1 tablespoon powder	6	11	1.2	.5	3.5
mix, with nonfat dry milk, 1 tablespoon powder	9	32	1.7	.2	6.4
mix, without milk, 1 tablespoon powder	9	31	.4	.2	8.0
mix, for hot chocolate, 1 tablespoon powder	9	35	.8	1.0	6.7
Coconut, fresh, meat only, 4 oz.	114	392	4.0	40.0	10.7
fresh, grated, 1 cup	80	277	2.8	28.2	7.5
fresh, shredded, 1 cup	98	339	3.4	34.6	9.2
dried, sweetened, 4 oz.	114	621	4.1	44.3	60.3
dried, sweetened, shredded, 1 cup	94	515	3.4	36.8	50.0
dried, unsweetened, shredded, 4 oz.	114	751	8.2	73.6	26.1
Coconut water (liquid from coconut), 1 cup	244	54	.7	.5	11.5
Cod, fresh, raw, 4 oz.	114	88	19.9	.3	0
fresh, broiled with butter, 4 oz.	114	194	32.5	6.0	0
canned, 4 oz.	114	97	21.9	.3	0
dehydrated, lightly salted, 4 oz.	114	428	93.9	3.2	0
dried, salted, 4 oz.	114	148	33.1	.8	0
frozen, cakes, reheated, 4 oz.	114	308	10.5	20.4	19.6
frozen, fillets, 4 oz. (2 average fillets)	114	84	18.8	.4	0
frozen, sticks, 4 oz. (5 average sticks)	114	276	15.1	10.7	29.1
Coffee, instant, dry, 1 teaspoon	2	3	tr.	tr.	.7
Coleslaw, commercial, with French dressing, 4 oz.	114	108	1.4	8.3	8.7
Collards, raw, with stems, 1 lb.	454	181	16.3	3.2	32.7
raw, leaves only, 1 lb.	454	139	14.8	2.5	23.1
boiled, drained, with stems, 1 cup	190	55	5.1	1.1	9.3
boiled, drained, leaves only, 1 cup	190	63	6.8	1.3	9.7
frozen, chopped, boiled, drained, 1 cup	170	51	4.9	.7	9.5
Cookies, commercial packaged:					
animal crackers, 1 oz.	28	122	1.9	2.7	22.7
assorted, 1 oz.	28	136	1.4	5.7	20.1

FOOD AND MEASURE	Weight (gm.)	Calories	Protein (gm.)	Fat (gm.)	Carbo-hydrate (gm.)
brownies, with nuts, iced, frozen, 1 oz.	28	119	1.4	5.8	17.2
butter, thin, rich, 1 oz.	28	130	1.7	4.8	20.1
chocolate, 1 oz.	28	126	2.0	4.5	20.3
chocolate chip, 1 oz.	28	134	1.5	5.9	19.8
coconut bar, 1 oz.	28	140	1.8	6.9	18.1
creme sandwich, 1 oz.	28	140	1.4	6.4	19.6
fig bar, 1 oz.	28	101	1.1	1.6	21.4
gingersnaps, 1 oz.	28	119	1.6	2.5	22.6
graham crackers, 1 oz.	28	109	2.3	2.7	20.8
graham crackers, chocolate coated, 1 oz.	28	135	1.4	6.7	19.2
ladyfingers, 1 oz.	28	102	2.2	2.2	18.3
macaroon, 1 oz.	28	135	1.5	6.6	18.7
marshmallow, 1 oz.	28	116	1.1	3.7	20.5
oatmeal, with raisins, 1 oz.	28	123	1.8	4.4	20.8
peanut, 1 oz.	28	134	2.8	5.4	19.0
raisin, 1 oz.	28	107	1.2	1.5	22.9
shortbread, 1 oz.	28	141	2.0	6.5	18.4
sugar wafers, 1 oz.	28	137	1.4	5.5	20.8
Cookies, baked from mix, brownies, made with nuts, 1 oz.	28	114	1.4	5.3	16.9
brownies, made with nuts, egg, 1 oz.	28	121	1.4	5.7	17.9
plain, made with egg, 1 oz.	28	140	1.4	6.9	18.4
plain, made with milk, 1 oz.	28	139	1.0	6.7	18.9
Cookie dough, refrigerated, baked, 1 oz.	28	141	1.1	7.1	18.4
Cookie crumbs, graham cracker, 1 cup	86	330	6.9	8.1	63.1
Corn, sweet, fresh, on cob, boiled, drained, 1 ear (5")	140	71	2.6	.8	16.4
fresh, kernels, boiled, drained, 1 cup	166	138	5.2	1.6	31.2
canned, kernels, boiled, drained, 1 cup	173	145	4.5	1.4	34.3
canned, kernels, vacuum-pack, 1 cup	212	176	5.3	1.1	43.5
canned, cream-style, 1 cup	253	207	5.3	1.5	50.6
frozen, on cob, 1 ear (3½ oz.)	100	82	3.1	.5	19.1

frozen, kernels, boiled, drained, 1 cup	182	144	5.5	.9	34.2
Corn bread mix, made with egg, milk, 2 oz.	57	132	3.6	4.8	18.7
Corn flour, 4 oz.	114	417	8.8	2.9	87.1
Corn grits, degermed, dry, ¼ cup	40	145	3.5	.3	31.2
Corn grits, degermed, cooked, 1 cup	242	123	2.9	2.4	26.6
Cornmeal, white or yellow, dry form, 4 oz.:					
whole ground, unbolted	114	403	10.4	4.4	83.6
bolted	114	411	10.2	3.9	84.5
degermed	114	413	8.9	1.4	88.9
self-rising, degermed	114	395	8.6	1.2	85.3
Cornmeal, cooked, 1 cup	240	120	2.6	.5	25.7
Corn muffin, baked from mix,					
made with egg, milk, 2 oz.	57	185	3.9	6.0	28.5
made with egg, water, 2 oz.	57	169	2.6	4.4	29.6
Cornstarch, 1 tablespoon	8	28	tr.	tr.	7.0
Cowpeas, immature seeds, raw,					
in pods, 1 lb.	454	317	22.5	2.0	54.4
raw, shelled, 1 lb.	454	576	40.8	3.6	98.9
fresh, boiled, drained, 1 cup	160	173	13.0	1.3	29.0
canned, with liquid, 4 oz.	114	80	5.7	.3	14.1
frozen, boiled, drained, 1 cup	142	185	12.6	.6	33.5
Cowpeas, mature seeds, cooked,					
1 cup	248	188	12.6	7.4	34.2
Crab, fresh, steamed in shell, 1 lb.	454	202	37.7	4.1	1.1
fresh, steamed, meat only, 4 oz.	114	105	19.6	2.2	.6
canned, meat only, 4 oz.	114	115	19.7	2.8	1.2
canned, meat only, 1 cup	170	172	29.6	4.2	1.9
Crabapples, raw, flesh only, 4 oz.	114	77	.5	.3	20.2
Cracker meal, 4 oz.	114	497	10.4	14.8	80.1
Crackers, commercial packaged:					
barbecue flavor, 1 oz.	28	142	1.9	7.5	18.0
butter, 1 oz.	28	130	2.0	5.0	19.1
cheese, 1 oz.	28	136	3.2	6.0	17.1
oyster, 1 oz.	28	112	2.8	2.8	19.8
peanut butter-cheese sandwich,					
1 oz.	28	139	4.3	6.8	15.9
saltines, 1 oz.	28	123	2.6	3.4	20.3
whole wheat, 1 oz.	28	114	2.4	3.9	19.3
zwieback, 1 oz.	28	121	2.8	2.8	21.8
Cranberries, fresh, whole, 1 lb.	454	200	1.7	3.0	47.0

27

FOOD AND MEASURE	Weight (gm.)	Calories	Protein (gm.)	Fat (gm.)	Carbo- hydrate (gm.)
Cranberries, fresh, without stems, 1 cup	115	53	.5	.8	12.4
Cranberry juice cocktail, bottled, 6-oz. glass	183	122	tr.	.2	31.0
Cranberry relish, with orange, uncooked, 1 cup	280	498	1.1	1.1	127.1
Cranberry sauce, canned, sweet, strained, 1 cup	271	396	.3	.5	101.6
Crayfish, raw, in shell, 1 lb.	454	39	7.9	.3	.7
Crayfish, raw, meat only, 1 lb.	454	327	66.2	2.3	5.4
Cream, dairy, half and half, 1 cup	242	324	7.7	28.3	11.1
half and half, 1 tablespoon	15	20	.5	1.8	.7
light, table or coffee, 1 cup	240	506	7.2	59.4	10.4
light, table or coffee, 1 tablespoon	15	32	.4	3.1	.6
whipping, light, 1 cup unwhipped	239	717	6.0	74.8	8.6
whipping, light, 1 tablespoon unwhipped	15	45	.4	4.7	.5
whipping, light, 1 tablespoon whipped	7	23	.2	2.4	.3
whipping, heavy, 1 cup unwhipped	238	837	5.2	89.4	7.4
whipping, heavy, 1 tablespoon unwhipped	15	53	.3	5.6	.5
whipping, heavy, 1 tablespoon whipped	7	27	.2	2.8	.3
Cream, sour, 1 cup	230	485	7.0	47.0	10.0
Cream, sour, 1 tablespoon	12	26	.3	2.0	1.0
Cream products, imitation: creamer, powdered, 1 tablespoon	6	30	.6	1.5	3.6
creamer, frozen, liquid, 1 tablespoon	15	20	tr.	2.0	2.0
sour cream, dressing, 1 tablespoon	12	20	tr.	2.0	1.0
Cress, garden, raw, untrimmed, 1 lb.	454	103	8.4	2.3	17.7
boiled in little water, drained, 1 cup	200	46	3.8	1.2	7.6

boiled in large amount water, drained, 1 cup	200	44	3.6	1.2	7.2
Cress, water, see Watercress					
Croaker, Atlantic, baked, 4 oz.	114	152	27.7	3.6	0
Cucumber, fresh, with skin, 1 medium, 7½″ × 2″	207	31	1.2	.2	6.9
fresh, pared, 1 medium, 7½″ × 2″	207	29	1.2	.2	6.6
fresh, sliced, pared, 6 slices, ⅛″ × 2″	50	7	.3	tr.	1.6
fresh, diced, pared, 1 cup	144	20	.9	.1	4.6
pickled, see Pickles					
Currants:					
black, fresh, with stems, 1 lb.	454	240	7.6	.4	58.2
black, fresh, without stems, 1 cup	114	60	1.9	.1	14.5
red or white, fresh, with stems, 1 lb.	454	220	6.2	.9	53.2
red or white, fresh, without stems, 1 cup	114	55	1.5	.2	13.3

D

Dandelion greens, boiled, drained, 1 cup	180	59	3.6	1.1	11.5
Dates, domestic, natural and dry:					
with pits, 4 oz.	114	270	2.2	.5	71.9
pitted, 4 oz.	114	311	2.5	.6	82.7
pitted, 4 average (about 1 oz.)	26	71	.8	.1	18.9
pitted, chopped, 1 cup	174	477	3.8	.9	126.8
pitted, chopped, 1 cup loose packed	142	389	3.1	.7	103.5
Dock or sorrel, raw, with stems, 1 lb.	454	89	6.7	1.0	17.8
Dock or sorrel, boiled, drained, 1 cup	200	38	3.2	.4	7.8
Doughnuts, cake type, 1 oz.	28	111	1.3	5.3	14.6
Doughnuts, cake type, 1 average	32	125	1.5	5.9	16.4
Doughnuts, yeast-leavened, 1 oz.	28	117	1.8	7.7	10.7
Duck, domestic, roasted, meat only, 4 oz.	114	352	25.8	26.7	0

E

Eel, domestic, raw, meat only, 4 oz.	114	264	18.0	20.7	0
Eel, smoked, 4 oz.	114	376	21.2	31.7	0

FOOD AND MEASURE	Weight (gm.)	Calories	Protein (gm.)	Fat (gm.)	Carbo-hydrate (gm.)
Eggs, chicken, raw, whole, 1 large	50	81	6.4	5.7	.4
raw, yolk from 1 large egg	17	59	2.7	5.2	.4
boiled, 1 large	50	81	6.4	5.7	.4
cooked with ½ tablespoon					
butter, 1 large	50	108	6.9	8.6	.2
poached, 1 large	50	81	6.3	5.8	.4
dried, whole, 2 tablespoons	14	83	6.6	5.8	.5
dried, whole, ½ cup	54	320	25.4	22.2	2.2
dried, white, powdered,					
2 tablespoons	14	52	11.2	tr.	.8
dried, yolk, powdered,					
2 tablespoons	14	93	4.6	7.9	.4
Eggnog, dairy-packaged, 6%					
butterfat, 1 cup	250	160	4.1	8.3	17.3
Eggnog, dairy-packaged, 8%					
butterfat, 1 cup	255	186	4.2	11.0	17.6
Eggplant, raw, whole, 1 lb.	454	92	4.4	.7	20.6
Eggplant, raw, diced, 1 cup	398	50	2.4	.4	11.2
Eggplant, boiled, drained, 1 cup	200	38	2.0	.4	8.2
Elderberries, raw, with stems,					
1 lb.	454	307	11.1	2.1	69.9
Elderberries, raw, without stems,					
4 oz.	114	82	2.9	.6	18.6
Endive, French or Belgian, fresh,					
whole, 1 lb.	454	80	6.8	.4	16.4
fresh, 10 small leaves	25	5	.4	tr.	1.0
fresh, cut, 1 cup	50	10	.8	tr.	2.0
Escarole, fresh, untrimmed, 1 lb.	454	80	6.8	.4	16.4
fresh, 4 large outer leaves	100	20	1.7	.1	4.1
fresh, 7 small leaves	20	4	.3	tr.	.8
fresh, shredded, 1 cup	71	14	1.2	.1	2.9

F

FOOD AND MEASURE	Weight (gm.)	Calories	Protein (gm.)	Fat (gm.)	Carbo-hydrate (gm.)
Farina, see Cereal, cooking-type					
Fennel leaves, raw, trimmed,					
4 oz.	114	32	3.2	.5	5.8
Figs, raw, 1 lb.	454	363	5.4	1.4	92.1
canned in heavy syrup, whole,					
1 cup	252	213	1.3	.5	55.2
canned, 3 figs, 2 tablespoons					
heavy syrup	115	96	.6	.2	25.0
dried, uncooked, 4 oz.	114	311	4.9	1.5	78.4

dried, uncooked, 1 large (2″ × 1″)	21	57	.9	.3	14.5
candied, 1 oz.	28	85	.9	tr.	20.9
Filberts or hazelnuts, shelled, 4 oz.	114	719	14.3	70.7	18.9
Filberts or hazelnuts, 10–12 nuts	15	95	1.9	9.4	2.5
Finnan haddie, flesh only, raw, 1 lb.	454	467	105.2	1.8	0
Fish, see individual listings					
Fish bites, breaded, frozen, cooked, 4 oz.	114	268	11.2	13.8	24.6
Fish cakes, breaded, frozen, cooked, 4 oz.	114	308	10.5	20.4	19.6
Fish flakes, canned, 1 oz.	28	31	7.0	.2	0
Fish flour (from whole fish), 1 oz.	28	95	22.1	.1	0
Fish flour (from fish fillets), 1 oz.	28	113	26.4	tr.	0
Fish sticks, breaded, frozen, cooked, 4 oz.	114	201	18.9	10.1	7.1
Flounder, raw, whole, 1 lb.	454	118	25.0	1.2	0
Flounder, fillets, raw, 4 oz.	114	89	18.9	.9	0
Flour (see also individual listings):					
buckwheat, whole grain, sifted, 1 cup	100	335	11.7	2.4	72.9
buckwheat, dark, sifted, 1 cup	100	333	11.7	2.5	72.0
buckwheat, light, sifted, 1 cup	100	347	6.4	1.2	79.5
carob or St. Johnsbread, 3½ oz.	100	180	4.5	1.4	80.7
rye, dark, stirred, 1 cup	127	415	20.7	3.3	86.5
rye, light, unsifted, 1 cup	100	357	9.4	1.0	77.9
soybean, defatted, stirred, 1 cup	120	391	56.4	1.8	45.7
soybean, defatted, sifted, 1 cup	100	326	47.0	.9	38.1
soybean, high fat, 3½ oz.	100	380	41.2	12.1	33.3
wheat, all-purpose, unsifted, 1 cup	126	458	13.2	1.3	95.9
wheat, all-purpose, sifted, 1 cup	115	419	12.1	1.2	87.5
wheat, bread, unsifted, 1 cup	123	449	14.5	1.4	91.9
wheat, bread, sifted, 1 cup	117	427	13.8	1.3	87.4
wheat, cake, unsifted, 1 cup	111	404	8.3	.9	88.1
wheat, gluten, unsifted, 1 cup	135	510	55.9	2.6	63.7
wheat, gluten, sifted, 1 cup	131	491	53.8	2.5	61.4
wheat, self-rising, unsifted, 1 cup	127	447	11.8	1.2	94.2
wheat, self-rising, sifted, 1 cup	106	373	9.8	1.1	78.7
wheat, whole, stirred, 1 cup	137	456	18.2	2.7	97.3

FOOD AND MEASURE	Weight (gm.)	Calories	Protein (gm.)	Fat (gm.)	Carbo-hydrate (gm.)
Frankfurters, raw, average, all samples, 4 oz.	114	350	14.2	31.3	2.0
raw, all meat, 4 oz.	114	336	14.9	28.9	2.8
raw, with cereal added, 4 oz.	114	281	16.3	23.4	.2
raw, with nonfat dry milk added, 4 oz.	114	340	14.9	29.0	3.9
cooked, all meat, 1 average (8 per lb.)	56	170	6.9	15.2	.9
canned, 4 oz.	114	251	15.2	20.5	.2
Frog's legs, raw, meat only, 4 oz.	114	83	18.6	.3	0
Fruit, see individual listings					
Fruit cocktail, canned, with heavy syrup, 8 oz.	227	173	.9	.3	44.7
with heavy syrup, 1 cup	256	195	1.0	.3	50.4
water pack, 8 oz.	227	84	.9	.3	22.0
Fruit for salad, canned, with heavy syrup, 8 oz.	227	170	.7	.3	44.0
with heavy syrup, 1 cup	246	185	.7	.2	47.7
water pack, 8 oz.	227	80	.9	.3	20.7
Fruit, mixed, frozen, sweetened, 8 oz.	227	250	1.0	.2	63.8
Fruit salad, dairy-packaged, unsweetened, 8 oz.	227	136	1.4	.4	29.8

G

Garlic, cloves, peeled, 5 average cloves	10	14	.6	tr.	3.1
Gelatin, unflavored, dry, 1 package	7	25	6.0	tr.	0
unflavored, dry, 1 tablespoon	10	33	8.5	tr.	0
flavored dessert mix, dry, 3-oz. package	85	315	8.0	0	74.8
flavored dessert mix, made with water, 1 cup	240	142	4.0	0	33.8
Gingerroot, fresh, 1 oz.	28	14	.4	.3	2.7
Ginger, candied, crystallized, 1 oz.	28	97	tr.	tr.	24.6
Goose, roasted, meat only, 4 oz.	114	266	38.6	11.2	0
Goose, roasted, meat and skin, 4 oz.	114	503	26.1	43.4	0
Gooseberries, fresh, 1 lb.	454	177	3.6	.9	44.0
fresh, 1 cup	150	59	1.2	.3	14.6

canned with heavy syrup, 8 oz.	227	204	1.1	.2	52.2
canned, water pack, 8 oz.	227	59	1.1	.2	15.0
Grapefruit, fresh, pink or red,					
½ medium (4½″ diameter)	285	58	.7	.1	15.1
pink or red, sections, 1 cup	200	80	1.0	.2	20.8
white, seeded, ½ medium					
(4½″ diameter)	285	52	.6	.1	13.8
white, seedless, ½ medium					
(4½″ diameter)	285	53	.7	.1	12.6
white, sections, 1 cup	200	80	1.0	.2	20.9
Grapefruit, canned, in syrup,					
1 cup	256	179	1.5	.3	45.6
Grapefruit, canned, water pack,					
1 cup	246	74	1.5	.2	18.7
Grapefruit juice, fresh, 6-oz. glass	185	72	.9	.1	16.9
canned, sweetened, 6-oz. glass	188	100	.9	.1	24.0
canned, unsweetened, 6-oz.					
glass	185	76	.9	.1	18.1
frozen, sweetened, diluted,					
6-oz. glass	175	82	.7	.2	19.9
frozen, unsweetened, diluted,					
6-oz. glass	175	72	.9	.2	17.2
Grapefruit peel, candied, 1 oz.	28	90	.1	.1	22.9
Grape juice, canned, 6-oz. glass	185	122	.4	tr.	30.7
frozen, sweetened, diluted,					
6-oz. glass	185	98	.4	tr.	24.6
Grape juice drink, canned,					
6-oz. glass	185	99	.3	tr.	25.3
Grapes, American type (Concord,					
Delaware, etc.):					
fresh, 1 lb.	454	197	3.7	2.9	44.9
fresh, whole, 1 cup	153	66	1.2	1.0	15.0
Grapes, European type (Malaga,					
Thompson seedless, etc.):					
fresh, 1 lb.	454	270	2.4	1.2	69.8
fresh, whole, 1 cup	160	95	.9	.4	24.6
Grapes, seedless, canned in heavy					
syrup, 1 cup	200	154	1.0	.2	40.0
Grapes, seedless, canned, water					
pack, 1 cup	200	102	1.0	.2	27.2
Grouper, raw, meat only, 4 oz.	114	99	21.9	.6	0
Guava, fresh, trimmed, 4 oz.	114	70	.9	.7	17.0
Guava, fresh, 1 small	80	48	.6	.5	11.7
Guinea hen, raw, whole,					
ready-to-cook, 1 lb.	454	594	88.0	24.4	0

FOOD AND MEASURE	Weight (gm.)	Calories	Protein (gm.)	Fat (gm.)	Carbo-hydrate (gm.)

H

FOOD AND MEASURE	Weight (gm.)	Calories	Protein (gm.)	Fat (gm.)	Carbo-hydrate (gm.)
Haddock, raw, meat only, 4 oz.	114	90	20.8	.1	0
fresh, fillet, breaded, fried, 3½ oz.	100	165	19.6	6.4	5.8
smoked, 4 oz.	114	117	26.3	.5	0
Halibut, Atlantic or Pacific, fresh, broiled with butter, 4 oz.	114	195	28.7	8.0	0
frozen, steak, 4 oz.	114	144	21.2	6.0	0
smoked, 4 oz.	114	254	23.6	17.0	0
Ham (meat only), boiled, 4 oz.	114	266	21.6	19.4	0
fresh, medium-fat, roasted, 4 oz.	114	426	26.2	34.8	0
light-cured, medium fat, roasted, 4 oz.	114	329	23.8	25.2	0
light-cured, lean, roasted, 4 oz.	114	213	28.8	10.0	0
long-cured, country style, medium fat, 4 oz.	114	443	19.3	39.9	0
long-cured, country style, lean, 4 oz.	114	353	22.2	28.5	0
picnic, medium fat, roasted, 4 oz.	114	368	25.5	28.7	0
picnic, lean, roasted, 4 oz.	114	241	32.4	11.3	0
Ham, deviled, canned, 2 oz.	57	200	7.8	18.4	0
Ham, spiced, canned, 2 oz.	57	168	8.5	14.2	.7
Headcheese, 4 oz.	114	305	17.7	25.1	1.1
Heart, fresh, beef, lean, braised, 4 oz.	114	214	35.7	6.5	.8
calf, braised, 4 oz.	114	237	31.7	10.4	2.0
chicken, simmered, 4 oz.	114	197	28.8	8.2	.1
lamb, braised, 4 oz.	114	296	33.6	16.4	1.1
turkey, simmered, 4 oz.	114	246	25.8	15.0	.3
Herring, Atlantic, raw, meat only, 4 oz.	114	200	19.6	12.8	0
Pacific, raw, meat only, 4 oz.	114	111	19.8	2.9	0
canned, with tomato sauce, 4 oz.	114	200	17.9	11.9	4.2
pickled, Bismark type, 4 oz.	114	253	23.1	17.1	0
salted or brined, 4 oz.	114	247	21.5	17.2	0
smoked, bloaters, 4 oz.	114	222	22.6	14.1	0
smoked, hard, 4 oz.	114	340	41.8	17.9	0
smoked, kippered, 4 oz.	114	239	25.2	14.6	0

Hickory nuts, shelled, 4 oz.	114	763	15.0	78.0	14.5
Honey, strained or extracted, 1 tablespoon	21	64	tr.	0	17.3
Honeydew melon, fresh, whole, 1 lb.	454	94	2.3	.9	22.0
1 wedge, 2" × 7"	150	49	1.2	.5	11.5
diced, 1 cup	168	55	1.3	.5	12.9
Horseradish, raw, pared, 1 oz.	28	25	.9	.1	5.6
Horseradish, prepared, 1 oz.	28	11	.4	.1	2.7

I

Ice cream and frozen custard:					
regular, about 10% fat, 1 cup	133	257	6.0	14.1	27.7
regular, about 12% fat, 1 cup	133	275	5.3	16.6	27.4
rich, about 16% fat, 1 cup	148	329	3.8	23.8	26.6
Ice cream cone, 1 average	5	19	.5	.1	3.9
Ice milk, hardened, 1 cup	131	199	6.3	6.7	29.3
Ice milk, soft-serve, 1 cup	175	266	8.4	8.9	39.2
Ices, water, lime, 1 cup	180	140	.7	tr.	58.7
Icing, cake, mix, made with water and table fat:					
chocolate fudge, 1 oz.	28	107	.6	4.1	19.0
creamy fudge, 1 oz.	28	109	.7	4.3	18.7

J

Jackfruit, raw, flesh only, 4 oz.	114	111	1.5	.3	28.8
Jams and preserves, all flavors, 1 tablespoon	20	54	.1	tr.	14.0
Jellies, all flavors, 1 tablespoon	20	55	tr.	tr.	14.3
Juices, see individual listings					
Jerusalem artichoke, raw, pared, 4 oz.	114	76	2.6	.1	18.9
Jujube (Chinese date), fresh, seeded, 4 oz.	114	119	1.4	.2	31.3
Jujube (Chinese date), dried, seeded, 4 oz.	114	325	4.2	1.2	83.5

K

Kale, raw, with stems, 1 lb.	454	128	14.1	2.7	20.1
raw, leaves only, 4 oz.	114	60	6.8	.9	10.2
boiled, drained, leaves and stems, 1 cup	110	31	3.5	.8	4.4
frozen, boiled, drained, 1 cup	184	57	5.5	.9	9.9
Kidney, beef, braised, 4 oz.	114	286	37.4	13.6	.9
Knockwurst, 4 oz.	114	317	16.1	26.4	2.5
Kohlrabi, raw, trimmed, 4 oz.	114	33	2.3	.1	7.5

35

FOOD AND MEASURE	Weight (gm.)	Calories	Protein (gm.)	Fat (gm.)	Carbo-hydrate (gm.)
Kohlrabi, boiled, drained, 1 cup	155	37	2.6	.2	8.2
Kumquats, fresh, with seeds, 4 oz.	114	74	1.0	.1	19.4
Kumquats, fresh, 4 average	60	39	.5	tr.	10.3

L

FOOD AND MEASURE	Weight (gm.)	Calories	Protein (gm.)	Fat (gm.)	Carbo-hydrate (gm.)
Lamb, fresh, choice grade:					
chop, loin, 4.8 oz. with bone, broiled, lean and fat	112	402	24.6	32.9	0
chop, loin, 4.8 oz. with bone, broiled, lean only	74	140	20.8	5.5	0
chop, rib, boned, broiled, lean and fat, 4 oz.	114	462	22.8	40.4	0
chop, rib, boned, broiled, lean only, 4 oz.	114	239	30.8	11.9	0
leg, roasted, lean and fat, 4 oz.	114	318	28.8	21.5	0
leg, roasted, lean only, 4 oz.	114	212	32.7	8.0	0
shoulder, roasted, lean and fat, 4 oz.	114	385	24.7	31.0	0
shoulder, roasted, lean only, 4 oz.	114	234	32.6	11.4	0
Lambsquarter, raw, fully trimmed, 1 lb.	454	195	19.1	3.6	33.1
Lambsquarter, boiled, drained, 1 cup	200	64	6.4	1.4	10.0
Lard, 1 cup	205	1849	0	205.0	0
Lard, 1 tablespoon	13	117	0	13.0	0
Leeks, raw, bulb and lower leaf, 4 oz.	114	59	2.5	.3	12.7
Leeks, raw, 3 average	100	52	2.2	.3	11.2
Lemonade, frozen, sweetened, diluted, 1 cup	242	106	.2	tr.	27.6
Lemon juice, unsweetened:					
fresh, ½ cup	123	31	.6	.2	9.8
fresh, 1 tablespoon	15	4	.1	tr.	1.2
canned or bottled, ½ cup	122	28	.5	.1	9.3
frozen, single-strength, ½ cup	122	27	.4	.2	8.8
Lemon peel, fresh, from 1 average lemon	34	n.a.	.5	.1	5.4

Lemon peel, candied, 1 oz.	28	88	.1	.1	22.6
Lemons, 1 average (2⅛″ diameter)	110	20	.8	.2	5.8
Lentils, whole, dry, 1 cup	190	646	46.9	2.1	114.2
whole, cooked, drained, 1 cup	202	214	15.8	tr.	39.0
split, dry, 4 oz.	114	391	28.0	1.0	70.1
Lettuce, fresh, Boston or bibb, 1 head (4″ diameter)	220	31	2.6	.4	5.5
iceberg, untrimmed, 1 lb. head (4¾″ diameter)	454	56	3.9	.4	12.5
iceberg, 3 average leaves	45	6	.4	tr.	1.3
iceberg, chunks, 1 cup	74	10	.7	.1	2.1
looseleaf or romaine, untrimmed, 1 lb.	454	52	3.8	.9	10.2
looseleaf, 2 large leaves	50	9	.6	.1	1.8
romaine, 3 leaves (8″ long)	28	5	.4	.1	1.0
Lichee nuts, dry, shelled, 6 average	15	41	.6	.2	10.6
Limeade, frozen, sweetened, diluted, 1 cup	247	101	tr.	tr.	27.2
Lime juice, fresh, unsweetened, ½ cup	123	32	.4	.1	11.1
Lime juice, fresh, unsweetened, 1 tablespoon	15	4	tr.	tr.	1.4
Limes, fresh, 1 average (1½″ long)	68	19	.5	.1	6.5
Liquor, see Alcoholic Beverages					
Liver, fresh, beef, fried, 4 oz.	114	260	29.9	12.0	6.0
calf, fried, 4 oz.	114	296	33.5	15.0	4.5
chicken, simmered, 4 oz.	114	187	30.1	5.0	3.5
lamb, broiled, 4 oz.	114	296	36.6	14.1	3.2
turkey, simmered, 4 oz.	114	197	31.6	5.4	3.5
Liverwurst, fresh, 4 oz.	114	350	18.5	29.2	2.0
Liverwurst, smoked, 4 oz.	114	364	16.9	31.2	2.6
Lobster, northern, fresh, cooked in shell, 1 lb.	454	112	22.0	1.8	.4
Lobster, northern, fresh or canned, meat only, 4 oz.	114	108	21.2	1.7	.3
Lobster paste, canned, 1 oz.	28	51	5.9	2.7	.4
Loganberries, fresh, trimmed, 1 cup	145	90	1.5	.9	21.6
canned, water pack, 4 oz.	114	45	.8	.5	10.7
canned, with heavy syrup, 4 oz.	114	101	.7	.5	25.2

37

FOOD AND MEASURE	Weight (gm.)	Calories	Protein (gm.)	Fat (gm.)	Carbo-hydrate (gm.)
M					
Macadamia nuts, shelled, 6 average nuts	15	104	1.2	10.7	2.4
Macaroni, cooked 8–10 minutes, drained, 1 cup	130	192	6.5	.6	39.1
Macaroni, cooked 14–20 minutes, drained, 1 cup	140	155	4.8	.6	32.2
Mackerel, Atlantic, broiled with butter, meat only, 4 oz.	114	268	24.7	17.9	0
Atlantic, canned with liquid, 4 oz.	114	208	21.9	12.6	0
Pacific, canned with liquid, 4 oz.	114	204	23.9	11.3	0
salted, meat only, 4 oz.	114	345	21.0	28.5	0
smoked, meat only, 4 oz.	114	248	27.0	14.7	0
Mangoes, fresh, whole, 1 average (3¾″ long)	303	134	1.4	.8	34.1
Mangoes, fresh, diced, 1 cup	163	108	1.1	.7	27.4
Margarine, 1 cup or ½ lb.	227	1633	1.4	183.5	.9
Margarine, 1 tablespoon	14	101	.1	11.3	tr.
Marmalade, citrus, 1 tablespoon	20	51	.1	tr.	14.0
Mayonnaise, see Salad Dressings					
Meat, see individual listings					
Melon, see individual listings					
Melon balls, in syrup, frozen, 8 oz.	227	141	1.4	.2	35.6
Milk, cow's, fresh, whole, 3.5% fat, 1 cup	244	159	8.5	8.5	11.9
whole, 3.7% butterfat, 1 cup	244	161	8.5	9.0	11.9
buttermilk, cultured, 1 cup	244	88	8.8	2.4	12.4
skim, 1 cup	246	88	8.8	.2	12.5
skim, partially (2% nonfat solids), 1 cup	246	145	10.3	4.9	14.8
Milk, canned, condensed, sweetened, ½ cup	153	491	12.4	13.3	83.1
Milk, canned, evaporated, unsweetened, 1 cup	126	173	8.8	9.9	12.2
Milk, dry, whole, 1 tablespoon powder	7	35	1.8	1.9	2.7
nonfat, regular, 1 cup powder	68	247	24.4	5.4	35.6
nonfat, instant, 1 cup powder	104	373	37.2	7.3	53.7

	Weight (gm.)	Calories			
buttermilk, cultured, 1 cup powder	120	464	41.2	6.4	60.0
Milk, chocolate, canned or dairy-packed:					
made with whole milk, 1 cup	250	213	8.5	8.5	27.5
made with skim milk, 1 cup	250	190	8.2	5.7	27.2
Mortadella, 4 oz.	114	359	23.2	28.5	.7
Mushrooms, raw, sliced, 1 cup	68	19	1.8	.2	3.0
Mushrooms, canned, with liquid, 1 cup	244	41	4.6	.2	5.9
Mussels, raw, meat only, 4 oz.	114	108	16.3	2.5	3.8
Mussels, canned, drained, 4 oz.	114	130	20.7	3.8	1.7
Mustard, prepared, brown, 1 teaspoon	10	9	.6	.6	.5
Mustard, prepared, yellow, 1 teaspoon	10	8	.5	.4	.6
Mustard greens, fresh, boiled, drained, 1 cup	221	51	4.9	.9	8.8
Mustard spinach, fresh, boiled, drained, 4 oz.	114	18	1.9	.2	3.2

N-O

Nectarines, fresh, 1 average (about 9 per lb.)	50	30	.3	tr.	7.9
Noodles, egg, cooked, 1 cup	160	200	6.6	2.4	37.3
Noodles, fried, chow-mein type, canned, 1 cup	45	220	5.9	10.6	26.1
Oatmeal, oats, see Cereals					
Ocean perch, Atlantic, raw, meat only, 4 oz.	114	100	20.4	1.4	0
Ocean perch, Pacific, raw, meat only, 4 oz.	114	108	21.6	1.7	0
Oil, cooking, salad or vegetable, 1 cup	210	1856	0	210.0	0
Oil, cooking, salad or vegetable, 1 tablespoon	14	124	0	14.0	0
Okra, fresh, slices, boiled, drained, 1 cup	160	46	3.2	.5	9.6
frozen, cuts, boiled, drained, 1 cup	184	70	4.0	.2	16.2
frozen, whole, boiled, drained, 1 cup	138	52	3.0	.1	12.1
Olives, canned or bottled, green, 2 oz.	57	66	.8	7.3	.8
ripe, Ascolano, Manzanilla, 2 oz.	57	73	.6	7.9	1.5

FOOD AND MEASURE	Weight (gm.)	Calories	Protein (gm.)	Fat (gm.)	Carbo-hydrate (gm.)
ripe, Mission, 2 oz.	57	105	.7	11.5	1.8
ripe, salt-cured, oil coated, Greek type, 2 oz.	57	193	1.2	20.4	4.9
Onions, green, fresh, bulb and white stem, 6 small	50	23	.6	.1	5.3
Onions, mature, fresh, 1 average (2½" diameter)	110	40	1.6	.1	9.6
raw, chopped, 1 cup	173	66	2.6	.2	15.1
raw, slices, 1 cup	113	43	1.7	.1	9.8
large, boiled, drained, halves, 1 cup	179	52	2.1	.2	11.6
pearl, boiled, drained, whole, 1 cup	185	54	2.2	.2	12.0
dehydrated, flakes, ½ cup	32	112	2.8	.4	2.6
Orange juice, fresh, average variety, 6-oz. glass	186	87	1.3	.4	20.2
canned, sweetened, 6-oz. glass	186	97	1.3	.4	22.7
canned, unsweetened, 6-oz. glass	186	89	1.5	.4	20.8
frozen, unsweetened, diluted, 6-oz. glass	186	84	1.3	.2	19.9
dehydrated, prepared, 6-oz. glass	186	85	1.1	.4	20.1
Orange-grapefruit juice, canned, sweetened, 6-oz. glass	185	93	.9	.2	22.6
canned, unsweetened, 6-oz. glass	185	79	1.1	.4	18.7
frozen, unsweetened, diluted, 6-oz. glass	175	77	1.0	.2	18.4
Orange peel, fresh, 1 oz.	28	n.a.	.4	.1	7.1
Orange peel, candied, 1 oz.	28	90	.1	.1	22.8
Oranges, fresh, California navel, 1 average (2⅘" diameter)	180	60	2.0	.2	16.0
California Valencia, whole, 1 lb.	454	174	4.1	1.0	42.2
Florida, 1 average (3" diameter)	210	75	1.5	.4	19.0
segments, 1 cup	195	94	2.0	.4	23.6
Oyster stew, see Soup					
Oysters, canned, with liquid, 4 oz.	114	87	9.7	2.5	5.6

	Weight (gms.)	Calories			
Pancakes, from mix, 4″ diameter cake:					
plain or buttermilk, prepared with milk	45	91	2.7	2.5	14.4
plain or buttermilk, prepared with milk and egg	45	101	3.2	3.3	14.6
Pancreas, beef, medium-fat, raw, 4 oz.	114	321	15.3	28.4	0
Parsley, fresh, chopped, 1 tablespoon	4	2	.1	tr.	.3
Parsnips, fresh, raw, pared, 4 oz.	114	86	1.9	.6	19.8
Parsnips, fresh, cuts, boiled, drained, 1 cup	211	139	3.2	1.1	31.4
Pastini, egg, dry, 2 oz.	57	217	7.3	2.3	40.7
Pâté de foie gras, canned, 1 tablespoon	14	65	1.6	6.1	.7
Peach nectar, canned, 6-oz. glass	185	89	.4	tr.	22.9
Peaches, fresh, 1 average (2″ diameter)	114	35	.7	.1	10.0
fresh, slices, 1 cup	177	67	1.1	.2	17.2
canned, water pack, 1 cup	245	76	1.0	.2	20.0
canned in heavy syrup, slices, 1 cup	253	197	1.0	.3	50.9
dehydrated, uncooked, 4 oz.	114	386	5.4	1.0	99.7
dried, uncooked, 4 oz.	114	297	3.5	.8	77.5
frozen, sweetened, slices, 8 oz.	227	200	9.1	.2	51.3
Peanut butter, 1 tablespoon	14	82	3.5	7.1	2.6
Peanuts, roasted, shelled, 4 oz.	114	660	29.7	55.2	23.4
roasted, shelled, 1 cup	144	842	37.4	71.7	27.0
roasted, chopped, 1 tablespoon	9	53	2.3	4.5	1.7
Pear nectar, canned, 6-oz. glass	185	96	.6	.4	24.4
Pears, fresh, 1 average (2½″ diameter)	182	101	1.2	.7	25.2
fresh, slices, 1 cup	164	100	1.1	.7	25.1
canned, water pack, 1 cup	244	78	.5	.5	20.3
canned in heavy syrup, halves, 1 cup	230	175	.5	.5	45.1
canned in heavy syrup, slices, 1 cup	255	194	.5	.5	38.0
dried, uncooked, 4 oz.	114	305	3.5	2.0	76.7
candied, 1 oz.	28	86	.4	.2	21.5
Peas, blackeye, see Cowpeas					
Peas, green, immature, raw, shelled, 1 cup	138	116	8.7	.6	19.9

FOOD AND MEASURE	Weight (gm.)	Calories	Protein (gm.)	Fat (gm.)	Carbo-hydrate (gm.)
fresh, boiled, drained, 1 cup	163	116	8.8	.7	19.7
early or June, canned, drained, 1 cup	172	151	8.1	.7	28.9
sweet, canned, drained, 1 cup	172	138	7.9	.7	25.8
frozen, boiled, drained, 1 cup	167	114	8.5	.5	19.7
Peas, dry, split, boiled, drained, 1 cup	194	223	15.5	.6	40.1
Peas and carrots, frozen, boiled, drained, 1 cup	174	92	5.6	.5	17.6
Pecans, shelled, 4 oz.	114	779	10.4	80.8	16.6
shelled, halves, 1 cup	108	742	9.9	76.9	15.8
shelled, chopped, 1 tablespoon	7	48	.6	5.0	1.0
Peppers, hot, chili, green, raw, seeded, 4 oz.	114	42	1.5	.2	10.3
green, pods, canned with liquid, 4 oz.	114	28	1.0	.1	6.9
red, raw, pods with seeds, 4 oz.	114	105	4.2	2.6	20.5
red, raw, pods, seeded, 4 oz.	114	74	2.6	.5	17.9
red, hot chili sauce, canned, 1 oz.	28	6	.3	.2	.1
red, dried pods, 1 tablespoon	8	26	1.0	.7	4.8
Peppers, sweet, green, raw, 1 average	62	14	.7	.1	3.0
green, raw, chopped, 1 cup	150	33	1.8	.3	7.2
green, raw, slices, 1 cup	82	18	1.0	.2	3.9
green, boiled, drained, 1 average	62	11	.6	.1	2.4
red, fresh, 1 average	60	19	.8	.2	4.3
Perch, white, raw, meat only, 4 oz.	114	134	21.9	4.5	0
Perch, yellow, raw, meat only, 4 oz.	114	103	22.1	1.0	0
Persimmons, Japanese or kaki, fresh, seedless, 4 oz.	114	87	.8	.5	22.3
Persimmons, native, fresh, flesh only, 4 oz.	114	144	.9	.5	38.0
Pheasant, raw, meat only, 4 oz.	114	184	26.8	7.7	0
Pickle relish, sour, 1 tablespoon	15	3	.1	.1	.4
Pickle relish, sweet, 1 tablespoon	15	21	.1	.1	5.1
Pickles, cucumber, dill, 1 average (4″ long)	133	15	.9	.3	2.9

fresh, bread and butter, 12 medium slices	100	73	.9	.2	17.9
sour, 1 average (4″ long)	133	13	.7	.3	2.6
sweet, 1 average (2¾″ long)	20	29	.1	.1	7.3
Pickles, chow-chow (with cauliflower), sour, 4 oz.	114	33	1.6	1.5	4.7
Pickles, chow-chow (with cauliflower), sweet, 4 oz.	114	132	1.7	1.0	30.6
Pie crust, mix, made with water, baked, 9″ shell	135	675	8.2	45.1	59.1
Pies, frozen, baked, apple, 2-oz. slice	57	145	1.1	5.8	22.8
cherry, 2-oz. slice	57	166	1.2	6.8	25.3
coconut custard, 2-oz. slice	57	142	3.4	6.8	16.8
Pignolia, see Pine nuts					
Pig's feet, pickled, 4 oz.	114	227	19.0	16.9	0
Pimientos, canned with liquid, 4 oz.	114	31	1.0	.6	6.6
Pimientos, canned, 1 average	38	10	.3	.2	2.2
Pineapple, raw, diced, 1 cup	140	73	.6	.3	19.2
canned, water pack, 4 oz.	114	44	.4	.1	11.6
canned, in juice, 4 oz.	114	66	.5	.1	17.1
canned, heavy syrup, crushed, 1 cup	262	194	.8	.3	50.8
canned, heavy syrup, 1 slice, 2 tablespoons syrup	122	90	.4	.1	23.7
canned, heavy syrup, tidbits, 1 cup	258	191	.8	.3	50.1
frozen, sweetened, chunks, 1 cup	230	196	1.0	.2	51.0
candied, 1 oz.	28	90	.2	.1	22.7
Pineapple juice, canned, unsweetened, 6-oz. glass	185	102	.7	.2	25.0
Pineapple juice, frozen, diluted, 6-oz. glass	175	91	.7	tr.	22.4
Pineapple-orange juice drink, canned, 6-oz. glass	185	100	.4	.2	25.0
Pine nuts, pignolia, shelled, 4 oz.	114	629	35.4	54.0	13.2
Pine nuts, piñon, shelled, 4 oz.	114	724	14.8	68.9	23.4
Pistachio nuts, shelled, 4 oz.	114	674	21.9	60.9	21.5
shelled, 1 cup	125	743	24.1	67.1	23.8
shelled, chopped, 1 tablespoon	9	53	1.7	4.8	1.7
Pizza with cheese, frozen, baked, 4 oz.	114	279	10.8	8.1	40.4
Plums, fresh, Damson, 1 average (2″ diameter)	60	36	.3	tr.	9.7

FOOD AND MEASURE	Weight (gm.)	Calories	Protein (gm.)	Fat (gm.)	Carbo-hydrate (gm.)
fresh, red hybrid, 1 average (2″ diameter)	60	27	.3	.1	6.9
fresh, red hybrid, pitted, halves, 1 cup	176	84	.9	.4	21.6
fresh, red hybrid, pitted, slices, 1 cup	169	81	.8	.3	20.8
fresh, prune-type, pitted, 4 oz.	114	85	.9	.2	22.3
canned, purple, water pack, 4 oz.	114	50	.4	.2	12.9
canned, purple, in heavy syrup, 1 cup	234	194	.9	.2	50.5
canned, greengage, water pack, 4 oz.	114	36	.4	.1	9.4
Pomegranate, fresh, pulp only, 1 average	100	63	.5	.3	16.4
Pompano, raw, meat only, 4 oz.	114	188	21.3	10.8	0
Popcorn, popped, plain, 1 cup	11	43	1.4	.6	8.4
popped, with oil or butter, 1 cup	14	64	1.4	3.1	8.3
popped, sugar-coated, 1 cup	18	69	1.1	.6	15.4
Porgy, raw, meat only, 4 oz.	114	127	21.6	3.9	0
Pork, fresh, medium-fat class: chop, broiled, lean and fat, 4 oz. with bone	114	297	18.6	23.6	0
chop, broiled, lean only, 4 oz. with bone	114	148	16.8	8.4	0
roast, Boston butt, cooked, lean and fat, 4 oz.	114	403	25.7	32.6	0
roast, Boston butt, cooked, lean only, 4 oz.	114	279	30.8	16.3	0
roast, loin, cooked, lean and fat, 4 oz.	114	414	28.0	32.6	0
roast, loin, cooked, lean only, 4 oz.	114	290	33.6	16.2	0
Pork, cured, see Ham					
Potato chips, 2 oz.	57	324	3.0	22.7	28.5
Potato sticks, 2 oz.	57	310	3.6	20.7	28.9
Potatoes, white, baked with skin, 1 small	100	93	2.6	.1	21.1
boiled with skin, 1 small	100	76	2.1	.1	17.1
boiled, peeled, 1 small	100	65	1.9	.1	14.5

boiled, drained, peeled, mashed, 1 cup	207	135	3.9	.2	30.0
canned, with liquid, 8 oz.	227	100	2.5	.5	22.2
French-fried, 10 pieces (2″ long)	57	156	2.4	7.5	20.5
frozen, French-fried, heated, 17 pieces	85	187	3.0	7.1	28.6
frozen, hash-browned, heated, 1 cup	200	448	4.0	23.0	58.0
dry flakes, mashed with water, milk, butter, 1 cup	200	186	3.8	6.4	29.0
dry granules, mashed with water, milk, butter, 1 cup	200	196	4.0	7.2	28.8
Potatoes, sweet, baked, 1 average	110	155	2.3	.5	35.7
boiled, 1 average	110	125	1.9	.5	28.9
boiled, drained, mashed, 1 cup	253	288	4.3	1.0	66.5
candied, 1 average (3½″ × 2¼″)	175	294	2.3	5.8	59.9
canned, vacuum or solid pack, 1 cup	218	235	4.4	.4	54.3
Pretzels, 2 oz.	57	222	5.6	2.6	43.3
Pretzels, 3-ring, small (7 per oz.)	4	16	.4	.2	3.0
Prickly pears, raw, flesh only, 4 oz.	114	48	.6	.1	12.4
Prune juice, canned or bottled, 6-oz. glass	192	148	.8	.2	36.5
Prunes, dehydrated, nugget-type, pitted, 4 oz.	114	390	3.8	.6	103.5
dehydrated, cooked, sweetened, pitted, 1 cup	251	452	3.0	.5	118.2
dried, "softenized," with pits, 4 oz.	114	246	2.0	.6	65.0
dried, with pits, cooked, sweetened, 1 cup	258	444	2.1	.5	116.4
dried, with pits, cooked, unsweetened, 1 cup	258	307	2.6	.8	81.0
Pudding, starch base, chocolate, with milk, 1 cup	290	360	9.8	8.8	66.1
starch base, chocolate, no-cook, with milk, 1 cup	300	376	9.0	7.4	73.2
vegetable gum base, custard, with milk, 1 cup	290	380	9.0	10.2	65.6
Pumpkin, fresh, pulp only, 4 oz.	114	30	1.1	.1	7.4
Pumpkin, canned, 1 cup	243	80	2.4	.7	19.2
Pumpkin seed kernels, dry, 4 oz.	114	630	33.0	53.2	17.0

FOOD AND MEASURE	Weight (gm.)	Calories	Protein (gm.)	Fat (gm.)	Carbo-hydrate (gm.)
Purslane leaves, boiled, drained, 1 cup	180	27	2.2	.6	5.0

R

FOOD AND MEASURE	Weight (gm.)	Calories	Protein (gm.)	Fat (gm.)	Carbo-hydrate (gm.)
Rabbit, domestic, stewed, 4 oz.	114	245	33.2	11.5	0
Radishes, fresh, 4 small	40	7	.4	tr.	1.4
Radishes, fresh, whole, 1 cup	132	22	1.3	.1	4.8
Radishes, fresh, slices, 1 cup	114	19	1.1	.1	4.1
Radishes, Oriental, pared, 4 oz.	114	22	1.0	.1	4.8
Raisins, natural, uncooked, 1 cup	143	413	3.6	.3	110.7
Raisins, cooked, sweetened, with liquid, 1 cup	243	517	2.9	.2	137.0
Raspberries, black, fresh, 1 cup	123	90	1.8	1.7	19.3
black, canned, unsweetened, with liquid, 8 oz.	227	116	2.5	2.5	24.3
red, fresh, 1 cup	140	80	1.7	.7	19.0
red, canned, unsweetened, with liquid, 8 oz.	227	79	1.6	.2	20.0
red, frozen, sweetened, 1 cup	249	244	1.6	.5	61.3
Rhubarb, raw, trimmed, 4 oz.	114	18	.7	.1	4.2
cooked, sweetened, with liquid, 1 cup	240	338	1.2	.2	86.4
frozen, sweetened, boiled, 1 cup	248	355	1.2	.4	89.8
Rice, brown, cooked, 1 cup	168	200	4.2	1.0	42.8
white, long grain, cooked, 1 cup	169	179	3.5	.2	39.4
white, precooked, ready-to-serve, 1 cup	140	153	3.1	tr.	33.9
Rolls, packaged, ready-to-serve, hard, 2 oz.	57	178	5.6	1.8	33.9
pan rolls, plain, 2 oz.	57	170	4.7	3.2	30.2
raisin, 2 oz.	57	157	3.9	1.6	32.1
sweet, 2 oz.	57	180	4.8	5.2	28.1
whole wheat, 2 oz.	57	146	5.7	1.6	29.8
Rolls, brown and serve, browned, 2 oz.	57	187	4.9	4.4	31.2
Rolls, mix, made with water, baked, 2 oz.	57	170	5.1	2.6	31.1

Salad dressing, bottled, French,				
1 tablespoon	15	62	.1	5.8	2.6
Italian, 1 tablespoon	15	83	tr.	9.0	1.0
mayonnaise, 1 tablespoon	15	108	.2	12.0	.3
Roquefort or blue cheese,				
1 tablespoon	15	76	.7	7.8	1.1
Russian, 1 tablespoon	15	74	.2	7.6	1.6
salad dressing, mayonnaise				
type, cooked, 1 tablespoon	15	65	.2	6.3	2.2
Thousand Island, 1 tablespoon	15	75	.1	7.5	2.3
Salami, dry, 4 oz.	114	513	27.1	43.4	1.4
Salami, cooked, 4 oz.	114	354	19.9	29.2	1.6
Salmon, Atlantic, canned with				
liquid, 4 oz.	114	232	24.8	13.9	0
Chinook or king, canned with				
liquid, 4 oz.	114	240	22.4	16.0	0
Chum, canned with liquid,				
4 oz.	114	159	24.5	5.9	0
Coho, canned with liquid,				
4 oz.	114	175	23.8	8.1	0
pink or humpback, canned				
with liquid, 4 oz.	114	161	23.4	6.7	0
red or sockeye, canned with				
liquid, 4 oz.	114	195	23.2	10.6	0
Salmon, smoked, 4 oz.	114	200	24.6	10.6	0
Salt pork, with skin, raw, 4 oz.	114	853	4.2	92.5	0
Sandwich spread, with chopped				
pickle, 1 tablespoon	15	57	tr.	5.4	2.4
Sapotes, fresh, flesh only, 4 oz.	114	142	2.0	.7	35.8
Sardines, Atlantic, canned in oil,				
drained, 3 oz.	85	173	20.4	9.4	n.a.
Pacific, canned with mustard,				
3½ oz.	100	196	18.8	12.0	1.7
Pacific, canned with brine or				
tomato sauce, 3½ oz.	100	197	18.7	12.2	1.7
Sauce, see individual listings				
Sauerkraut, canned, with liquid,				
4 oz.	114	20	1.1	.2	4.6
Sauerkraut juice, canned, ½ cup	114	11	.8	tr.	2.6
Sausage (see also individual				
listings):				
blood, 4 oz.	114	449	16.1	42.1	.3
brown-and-serve, browned,				
4 oz.	114	481	18.8	43.1	3.2

FOOD AND MEASURE	Weight (gm.)	Calories	Protein (gm.)	Fat (gm.)	Carbo-hydrate (gm.)
country-style, smoked, 4 oz.	114	393	17.2	35.4	0
Polish-style, 4 oz.	114	346	17.9	29.4	1.4
pork, links or bulk, cooked, 4 oz.	114	543	20.6	50.4	tr.
pork, canned, drained, 4 oz.	114	434	20.9	37.4	2.2
scrapple, 4 oz.	114	245	10.0	15.5	16.6
Vienna, canned, 4 oz.	114	274	16.0	22.6	.3
Scallops, bay or sea, fresh, steamed, 4 oz.	114	128	26.4	1.6	n.a.
Scallops, frozen, breaded, fried, reheated, 4 oz.	114	221	20.5	9.6	12.0
Sesame seeds, dry, hulled, 4 oz.	114	660	20.7	60.6	20.0
Shad, canned with liquid, 4 oz.	114	172	19.2	10.0	0
Shad roe, broiled with butter, lemon juice, 4 oz.	114	143	24.9	3.2	1.9
Shallots, fresh, peeled, 1 oz.	28	20	.7	tr.	4.8
Sherbet, orange, 1 cup	170	228	1.5	2.0	52.4
Shrimp, fresh, breaded, fried, 4 oz.	114	255	23.0	12.2	11.3
canned, with liquid, 4 oz.	114	91	18.4	.9	.9
canned, dry pack or drained, 4 oz.	114	132	27.4	1.2	.8
Shrimp paste, canned, 1 oz.	28	51	5.9	2.7	.4
Smelt, Atlantic, canned with liquid, 4 oz.	114	227	20.9	15.3	0
Snapper, red and grey, raw, meat only, 4 oz.	114	106	22.5	1.0	0
Soft drinks, carbonated, cola, 8-oz. glass	245	96	0	0	24.5
cream soda, 8-oz. glass	245	105	0	0	26.9
fruit-flavored soda, 8-oz. glass	245	113	0	0	29.4
ginger ale and quinine water, 8-oz. glass	245	76	0	0	19.6
root beer, 8-oz. glass	245	100	0	0	25.7
Sole, raw, fillets, 4 oz.	114	89	18.9	.9	0
Soup, condensed, diluted with equal amount water or milk, 1 cup:					
asparagus, cream of, diluted with milk	238	143	6.7	5.7	16.2
bean with pork, diluted with water	249	167	8.0	5.7	21.7

beef broth, bouillon or consommé, with water	238	31	5.0	0	2.6
beef noodle, diluted with water	238	67	3.8	2.6	6.9
chicken consommé, diluted with water	238	21	3.3	tr.	1.9
chicken, cream of, diluted with milk	238	174	7.1	10.0	14.0
chicken noodle, diluted with water	238	62	3.3	1.9	7.9
chicken with rice, diluted with water	238	48	3.1	1.2	5.7
chicken vegetable, diluted with water	240	74	4.1	2.4	9.4
clam chowder, Manhattan, diluted with water	240	79	2.2	2.4	12.0
clam chowder, New England, frozen, diluted with milk	235	202	8.7	11.8	15.7
minestrone, diluted with water	240	103	4.8	3.4	13.9
onion, diluted with water	238	64	5.2	2.4	5.2
oyster stew, frozen, diluted with milk	235	197	9.9	11.5	13.9
pea, green, diluted with water	245	130	5.6	2.2	22.5
pea, split, diluted with water	240	142	8.4	3.1	20.2
potato, cream of, frozen, diluted with milk	235	179	7.5	9.2	17.6
shrimp, cream of, frozen, diluted with milk	235	233	8.9	15.7	14.6
tomato, diluted with water	240	86	1.9	2.4	15.4
vegetable beef, diluted with water	240	77	5.0	2.2	9.4
vegetarian vegetable, diluted with water	240	77	2.2	1.9	13.0
Soy sauce, 1 tablespoon	14	9	.8	.2	1.2
Soybean curd or tofu, 4 oz.	114	82	8.9	4.8	2.7
Soybeans, young seeds, boiled, drained, 4 oz.	114	134	11.1	5.8	11.5
Spaghetti, cooked firm, 8–10 minutes, 1 cup	130	192	6.5	.7	39.1
cooked tender, 14–20 minutes, 1 cup	140	155	4.8	.6	32.2
canned in tomato sauce with cheese, 8 oz.	227	172	5.0	1.4	34.9
canned with meatballs and tomato sauce, 8 oz.	227	234	11.1	9.3	25.9

FOOD AND MEASURE	Weight (gm.)	Calories	Protein (gm.)	Fat (gm.)	Carbo-hydrate (gm.)
Spinach, fresh, raw, chopped, 1 cup	52	14	1.7	.2	2.2
fresh, boiled, drained, 1 cup	156	36	4.7	.5	5.6
canned, drained solids, 1 cup	223	54	6.0	1.3	8.0
frozen, leaf, boiled, drained, 1 cup	188	45	5.5	.6	7.3
frozen, chopped, boiled, drained, 1 cup	188	43	5.6	.6	7.0
Squash, summer, fresh, white, cooked, mashed, 1 cup	238	38	1.7	.2	9.0
yellow, boiled, drained, slices, 1 cup	176	26	1.8	.4	5.5
zucchini, boiled, drained, slices, 1 cup	152	18	1.5	.2	3.8
Squash, winter, fresh, acorn, baked, mashed, 1 cup	205	113	3.9	.2	28.7
butternut, baked, mashed, 1 cup	205	139	3.7	.2	35.9
hubbard, baked, mashed, 1 cup	205	102	3.7	.8	24.0
Strawberries, fresh, whole, capped, 1 cup	144	53	1.0	.7	12.1
frozen, sweetened, sliced, 8 oz.	227	247	1.2	.5	63.1
frozen, sweetened, whole, 8 oz.	227	209	.9	.5	53.3
Sturgeon, fresh, cooked, steamed, 4 oz.	114	181	28.8	6.5	0
Sturgeon, smoked, 4 oz.	114	169	35.4	2.1	0
Succotash, frozen, boiled, drained, 1 cup	192	179	8.1	.8	39.4
Sugar, brown, firm-packed, 1 cup	212	791	0	0	204.4
brown, firm-packed, 1 tablespoon	14	52	0	0	13.5
granulated, 1 cup	195	751	0	0	194.0
granulated, 1 tablespoon	12	46	0	0	12.0
powdered confectioners', stirred, 1 tablespoon	8	31	0	0	8.0
Sunflower seeds, hulled, 4 oz.	114	635	27.2	53.7	22.6
Sweetbreads, beef, braised, 4 oz.	114	363	29.4	26.3	0
Sweetbreads, calf, braised, 4 oz.	114	191	37.0	3.6	0

Syrups (see also individual listings):				
cane, 1 tablespoon	20	53	0	0	13.6
maple, 1 tablespoon	20	50	0	0	13.0
table blend, chiefly corn syrup, 1 tablespoon	20	58	0	0	15.0

T

Tangerine juice, fresh, 6-oz. glass	186	80	.9	.4	18.8
Tangerine juice, frozen, sweetened, diluted, 6-oz. glass	170	78	.9	.3	18.4
Tangerines, fresh, whole, 1 average (2½″ diameter)	114	39	.7	.2	9.7
Tangerines, fresh, sections only, 1 cup	193	89	1.5	.4	22.4
Tartare sauce, 1 tablespoon	14	74	.2	8.1	.6
Tea, instant, 1 teaspoon dry	4	1	n.a.	tr.	.4
Thuringer, 4 oz.	114	348	21.1	27.8	1.8
Tomato juice, canned, 6-oz. glass	181	34	1.6	.2	7.8
Tomato juice cocktail, canned, 6-oz. glass	181	38	1.3	.2	9.1
Tomato paste, canned, 1 cup	258	212	8.8	1.0	48.0
Tomato purée, canned, 1 cup	250	98	4.2	.5	22.3
Tomatoes, ripe, fresh, whole, 1 small (2½″ diameter)	150	33	1.6	.3	7.0
fresh, slices, 1 cup	181	40	2.0	.4	8.5
fresh, boiled, with liquid, 1 cup	242	62	3.2	.4	13.4
canned, with liquid, 1 cup	240	50	2.4	.5	10.3
Tongue, beef, fresh, medium-fat, braised, 4 oz.	114	277	24.4	18.9	.5
smoked, 4 oz.	114	n.a.	19.5	32.7	n.a.
canned or pickled, whole, 4 oz.	114	303	21.9	23.0	.3
potted or deviled, 4 oz.	114	329	21.1	26.1	.8
Tripe, beef, pickled, 4 oz.	114	70	13.4	1.5	0
Tuna fish, canned in oil, drained, 4 oz.	114	223	27.8	7.9	0
Tuna fish, canned in water, with liquid, 4 oz.	114	144	31.8	.9	0
Turkey, fresh, dark meat only, roasted, 4 oz.	114	232	34.3	9.5	0
Turkey, fresh, light meat only, roasted, 4 oz.	114	201	37.6	4.4	0
Turkey, fresh, skin only, roasted, 2 oz.	57	256	9.6	23.8	0

51

FOOD AND MEASURE	Weight (gm.)	Calories	Protein (gm.)	Fat (gm.)	Carbo-hydrate (gm.)
Turkey, canned, boned, 4 oz.	114	231	23.9	14.3	0
Turkey, potted, 4 oz.	114	283	9.9	21.9	0
Turkey pot pie, frozen, 8-oz. pie	227	447	13.2	23.6	45.6
Turnip greens, frozen, boiled, drained, 1 cup	163	37	4.1	.5	6.4
Turnips, fresh, raw, slices, 1 cup	127	36	3.8	.4	6.4
Turnips, fresh, boiled, drained, mashed, 1 cup	228	45	5.0	.5	7.7
Turtle, green, canned, 4 oz.	114	120	26.5	.8	0

V-W-Y-Z

FOOD AND MEASURE	Weight (gm.)	Calories	Protein (gm.)	Fat (gm.)	Carbo-hydrate (gm.)
Veal, fresh, flank, stewed, lean and fat, 4 oz.	114	446	27.2	36.9	0
loin, chop, broiled, lean and fat, meat only, 4 oz.	114	267	30.2	15.3	0
rib, roasted, lean and fat, meat only, 4 oz.	114	305	30.8	19.2	0
round with rump, broiled, lean and fat, 4 oz.	114	245	30.7	12.6	0
Vegetable juice cocktail, canned, 6-oz. glass	181	31	1.6	.2	6.5
Vegetables, see individual listings					
Vegetables, mixed, frozen, boiled, drained, 1 cup	182	116	5.8	.5	24.4
Vinegar, cider, 1 tablespoon	15	2	tr.	0	.9
Vinegar, distilled, 1 tablespoon	15	2	n.a.	n.a.	.8
Waffles, frozen, 1 double waffle	50	127	3.6	3.1	21.0
Walnuts, black, shelled, 4 oz.	114	712	23.3	67.3	16.8
black, shelled, chopped, 1 tablespoon	8	50	1.6	4.7	1.2
English, shelled, 4 oz.	114	738	16.8	72.6	17.9
English, shelled, chopped, 1 tablespoon	8	52	1.2	5.1	1.3
Water chestnuts, Chinese, raw, peeled, 4 oz.	114	90	1.6	.2	21.5
Watercress, fresh, trimmed, leaves and stems, 1 cup	33	6	.7	.1	1.0

Food	Weight (g)	Calories	Protein	Fat	Carbohydrate
Watermelon, fresh, whole, 1 wedge (4″ × 8″; about 2 lbs.)	925	111	2.1	.8	27.2
Watermelon, fresh, flesh only, diced, 1 cup	160	42	.8	.3	10.2
Weakfish, broiled, meat only, 4 oz.	114	236	27.9	12.9	0
Wheat bran, commercially milled, 4 oz.	114	412	30.2	12.4	53.0
Wheat germ, crude, commercially milled, 4 oz.	114	396	14.6	1.3	83.4
Whitefish, lake, smoked, meat only, 4 oz.	114	176	23.7	8.3	0
White sauce, standard home recipe, medium, 1 cup	255	413	9.9	31.9	22.4
Yeast, baker's, compressed, 1 cake	22	19	2.7	.1	2.4
Yeast, baker's, dry, 1 tablespoon or 1 package	7	20	2.6	.1	2.7
Yogurt, partially skim milk, 1 cup	249	125	8.5	4.2	12.9
Yogurt, whole milk, 1 cup	246	153	7.4	8.4	12.1
Zucchini, see Squash, summer					

Low-Calorie Menus

Here's a week's worth of 1200-calorie-a-day menus, all deliciously varied and nutritiously balanced. The dishes marked with asterisks are included in the section of low-calorie recipes.

Note: Portions are average size unless otherwise indicated; T. = 1 tablespoon, t. = teaspoon.

	Monday	Calories
Breakfast	Tomato Juice (½ cup)	23
	Boiled or Poached Egg	80
	Slice Whole Wheat Toast, 1 t. butter	98
	Black Coffee or Tea with Lemon	0
		201
Lunch	Cold Roast Beef and Tomato Sandwich (2 thin slices lean beef, ½ tomato, mustard or horseradish)	278
	Apple	70
	Skim Milk (1 cup)	90
		438
Dinner	Sautéed Calf's Liver*	280
	Riced Boiled Medium-Size Potato	100
	Asparagus	40
	Low-Calorie Sherbet	65
	Black Coffee or Tea with Lemon	0
		485
Anytime Snack	1 Cup Skim Milk	90
Total Day's Calories:		**1214**

	Tuesday	Calories
Breakfast	Orange Juice (½ cup)	55
	Ready-to-Eat High-Protein Cereal (1 cup with 1 t. sugar, ½ cup skim milk)	170
	½ Toasted English Muffin, 2 t. jelly	95
	Black Coffee or Tea with Lemon	0
		320
Lunch	Beef Broth (1 cup)	35
	Cottage Cheese (1 cup, uncreamed)	195
	½ Tomato on Lettuce (topped with minced scallions, 1 T. Tangy Low-Calorie Salad Dressing*)	45
	1 (2″) piece Angel Food Cake* (unfrosted)	120
	Black Coffee or Tea with Lemon	0
		395
Dinner	Egg Roll (packaged)	53
	Chicken Chow Mein*, ⅓ cup Boiled Rice	292
	Pineapple Chunks (½ cup water-pack)	64
	Vanilla Wafer (1)	20
	Black Coffee or Tea with Lemon	0
		429
Anytime Snack	½ Cup Skim Milk	45
Total Day's Calories:		**1189**

	Wednesday	Calories
Breakfast	½ Grapefruit	55
	1 Slice French Toast (fried in 1 t. butter, sprinkled with 1 t. confectioners' sugar)	198
	Black Coffee or Tea with Lemon	0
		253
Lunch	Tuna Sandwich (⅓ cup water-pack tuna mixed with minced celery, onion, lemon juice)	270
	Carrot and Celery Sticks	25
	Sliced Canned Peaches (½ cup water-pack)	38
	Skim Milk (1 cup)	90
		423
Dinner	Broiled (4 oz.) Herb Burger	247
	On ½ Toasted Bun	70
	Skillet Mushrooms	30
	Green Beans	35
	Broiled ½ Tomato	18
	Gingered Orange Fluff* with Low-Calorie Dessert Topping*	39
	Black Coffee or Tea with Lemon	0
		439
Anytime Snack	1 Cup Skim Milk	90
Total Day's Calories:		**1205**

	Thursday	Calories
Breakfast	Tomato Juice (½ cup)	23
	Boiled or Poached Egg	80
	Slice Whole Wheat Toast, 1 t. butter	98
	Black Coffee or Tea with Lemon	0
		201
Lunch	Clam Chickee*	20
	Chef's Salad (2 oz. cheese, 1 oz. lean ham, Low-Calorie Thousand Island Dressing)	305
	Melba Toast (2 slices)	32
	Skim Milk (1 cup)	90
		447
Dinner	Cabbage Rolls and Sauerkraut	270
	Poppy Seed Noodles (½ cup)	100
	Fruit Cocktail (½ cup water-pack)	72
	Vanilla Wafer (1)	20
	Black Coffee or Tea with Lemon	0
		462
Anytime Snack	1 Cup Skim Milk	90
Total Day's Calories:		**1200**

	Friday	Calories
Breakfast	Peach Nectar (½ cup)	60
	Ready-to-Eat High Protein Cereal (1 cup with	
	1 t. sugar, ½ cup skim milk)	170
	Black Coffee or Tea with Lemon	0
		230
Lunch	Tomato Cocktail*	35
	Scrambled Egg Sandwich (2 eggs scrambled in	
	2 t. butter, seasoned with chives)	333
	Skim Milk (1 cup)	90
		458
Dinner	Fillets of Flounder en Papillote*	180
	Medium-Size Parsleyed Potato	100
	Boiled Carrots	40
	Gingered Honeydew Melon*	65
	Black Coffee or Tea with Lemon	0
		385
Anytime	½ Cup Skim Milk	45
Snack	1 Small Banana	81
Total Day's Calories:		**1199**

	Saturday	Calories
Breakfast	½ Grapefruit	55
	Boiled or Poached Egg	80
	Slice Whole Wheat or Enriched Bread Toast,	
	1 t. butter	98
	Black Coffee or Tea with Lemon	0
		233
Lunch	Open-Face Grilled Cheese and Bacon Sandwich	269
	Wilted Cucumbers*	40
	Seedless Grapes (⅔ cup)	47
	Skim Milk (1 cup)	90
		446
Dinner	Steak Florentine* (4 oz.)	310
	Boiled Chopped Spinach	23
	Strawberries Grand Marnier*	100
	Black Coffee or Tea with Lemon	0
		433
Anytime	2 Medium-Size Carrots	40
Snack	½ Cup Skim Milk	45

Total Day's Calories: **1197**

	Sunday	Calories
Brunch	½ Medium-Size Cantaloupe	60
	2 Poached Eggs and 2 Slices Grilled Bacon	278
	Toasted English Muffin, 2 t. butter	206
	Black Coffee or Tea with Lemon	0
		544
Mid-Afternoon Snack	1 Medium-Size Apple	70
	1 Cup Skim Milk	90
		160
Dinner	½ Lemon-Broiled Chicken (small)	290
	Cauliflower	35
	Frozen French-Style Green Beans and Mushrooms (½ cup)	26
	Green Grapes and Sour Cream* (made with yogurt)	138
	Black Coffee or Tea with Lemon	0
		489

Total Day's Calories: **1193**

Low-Calorie Recipes

Whether it's a warming winter stew or some refreshing marinated artichoke hearts, meat loaf or baked custard; soup to nuts, a *low-calorie* recipe need not be a *dull* recipe. Just put fruit in the soup, oats in the meat loaf, buttermilk in the salad dressing, and then dry-roast your mushrooms till nutty! Select from the following recipes to create your own low-calorie menu with a difference.

Appetizers

TOMATO COCKTAIL

Makes 4 servings

1 pint tomato juice
2 tablespoons lemon juice
1 tablespoon sugar
1 tablespoon minced yellow onion
1 bay leaf, crumbled
Pinch pepper

Mix all ingredients, cover, and chill 1–2 hours. Strain and serve in juice glasses. About 35 calories per serving.

VARIATIONS:

Tomato-Celery Cocktail: Prepare as directed but add ½ cup diced celery and substitute 1 tablespoon cider vinegar for 1 tablespoon of the lemon juice. About 35 calories per serving.

Spicy Tomato Cocktail: Prepare as directed but add 1 teaspoon prepared horseradish, 1 crushed clove garlic, ½ teaspoon Worcestershire sauce and substitute minced scallions for yellow onion. About 35 calories per serving.

CLAM CHICKEE

Makes 4 servings

Mix 1 cup each chilled clam juice and chicken broth. Season to taste with celery salt and top each serving with a dollop of sour cream; sprinkle with salt and paprika. *Variation:* Substitute madrilène for chicken broth. About 20 calories per serving without cream.

DRY-ROASTED HERBED MUSHROOMS

An unusual appetizer and oh! so low in calories.
Makes 4–6 servings

> ½ *teaspoon garlic salt*
> 1 *pound medium-size mushrooms, wiped*
>   *clean and sliced thin*
> 1 *teaspoon seasoned salt*
> ½ *teaspoon oregano*
> ½ *teaspoon powdered rosemary*

Preheat oven to 200° F. Sprinkle 2 *lightly* oiled baking sheets with garlic salt and arrange mushrooms 1 layer deep on sheets. Mix seasoned salt and herbs and sprinkle evenly over mushrooms. Bake, uncovered, about 1½ hours until dry and crisp but not brown. Cool slightly and serve as a cocktail nibble. (*Note:* Store airtight; these absorb moisture rapidly.) About 30 calories for each of 4 servings, 20 for each of 6.

CAPONATA
(Sicilian Eggplant Spread)

Makes about 3 cups

> 4 *tablespoons olive oil*
> 1 *small eggplant, cut in 1" cubes but not peeled*
> 1 *medium-size yellow onion, peeled and minced*
> ⅓ *cup minced celery*
> 1 *cup tomato purée*
> ⅓ *cup coarsely chopped, pitted green and/or*
>   *ripe olives*

4 anchovy fillets, minced
2 tablespoons capers
2 tablespoons red wine vinegar
1 tablespoon sugar
½ teaspoon salt (about)
¼ teaspoon pepper
1 tablespoon minced parsley

Heat 3 tablespoons oil in a large, heavy saucepan 1 minute over moderately high heat, add eggplant and sauté, stirring now and then, 10 minutes until golden and nearly translucent. Add remaining oil, onion, and celery and stir-fry 5–8 minutes until pale golden. Add remaining ingredients except parsley, cover, and simmer 1¼–1½ hours until quite thick, stirring now and then. Mix in parsley, cool to room temperature, taste for salt and adjust as needed. Serve as a spread for crackers. About 17 calories per tablespoon.

CHEESE CRACKERS

Makes 6–7 dozen

1½ cups sifted flour
1 teaspoon salt
⅛ teaspoon paprika
⅛ teaspoon cayenne pepper
½ cup chilled margarine (no substitute)
½ pound sharp Cheddar cheese, coarsely
   grated
2½–3 tablespoons ice water

Mix flour, salt, paprika, and cayenne in a shallow bowl and cut in margarine with a pastry blender until mixture resembles coarse meal. Add cheese and toss to mix. Sprinkle water evenly over surface, 1 tablespoon at a time, mixing lightly with a fork; dough should just hold together. Divide dough in half and shape each on a lightly floured board into a roll about 9″ long and 1½″ in diameter; wrap in foil and chill well. About 10 minutes before crackers are to be baked, heat oven to 375° F. Slice rolls ¼″ thick, space 1″ apart on ungreased baking sheets, and bake 10 minutes until golden; transfer at once to wire racks to cool. Store airtight. Serve at room temperature or, if you prefer, reheat about 5 minutes at 350° F. About 30 calories per cracker.

PROSCIUTTO-STUFFED
MUSHROOM HORS D'OEUVRE

Makes 3½–4 dozen hors d'oeuvres

> 1 (3-ounce) package cream cheese,
>   softened to room temperature
> ½ (2-ounce) tube anchovy paste
> ¼ pound prosciutto, finely chopped
> 1 tablespoon capers
> 1 tablespoon minced parsley
> 1 tablespoon minced watercress
> ½ teaspoon Worcestershire sauce
> 3–4 tablespoons light cream
> 1 pound 1" mushrooms, stemmed and
>   peeled (save stems to use later)

Mix cheese, anchovy paste, prosciutto, capers, parsley, watercress, and Worcestershire, adding enough cream to give mixture the consistency of *pâté*. Stuff mushroom caps, heaping mixture in center, cover, and refrigerate until about ½ hour before serving. Let come to room temperature, then serve with cocktails. About 20 calories per hors d'oeuvre.

Soups

ANDALUSIAN GAZPACHO
(Cold Spanish Vegetable Soup)

Glorious on a hot summer day. And almost a meal in itself.
Makes 6 servings

> ¾ cup soft white bread crumbs
> 3 tablespoons red wine vinegar
> 2 cloves garlic, peeled and crushed
> ¼ cup olive oil
> 1 large cucumber, peeled, seeded, and
>   cut in fine dice

1 sweet green pepper, cored, seeded, and
   minced
8 large ripe tomatoes, peeled, cored,
   seeded, and chopped fine
1 cup cold water
½ teaspoon salt
⅛ teaspoon pepper

Place bread crumbs, vinegar, garlic, and oil in a small bowl and mix vigorously with a fork to form a smooth paste; set aside. Mix all remaining ingredients in a large mixing bowl, then blend in bread paste. Cover and chill at least 24 hours before serving. Serve icy cold in soup bowls as a first course or as a midafternoon refresher. For a special touch, bed the soup bowls in larger bowls of crushed ice and garnish with sprigs of fresh dill or basil or, failing that, watercress or parsley. About 130 calories per serving.

FRESH TOMATO SOUP
Makes 6 servings

2 medium-size yellow onions, peeled and quartered
1 stalk celery, cut in 2" chunks
1 (10½-ounce) can condensed beef consommé
6 large ripe tomatoes, peeled, cored, and quartered
1 tablespoon butter or margarine
2 teaspoons salt
⅛ teaspoon pepper
2 tablespoons minced fresh chives or dill

Place onions, celery, and consommé in a large saucepan, cover, and simmer 45 minutes until onions are mushy. Add tomatoes, cover, and simmer 15–20 minutes until tomatoes have reduced to juice; cool 10 minutes, then put through a food mill or purée, a little at a time, in an electric blender at low speed. Return to pan, add butter, salt, and pepper, and simmer uncovered 5 minutes. Serve hot or cold garnished with minced chives. About 75 calories per serving.

ARTICHOKE SOUP

An unusually delicate soup. Good hot or cold.
Makes 4 servings

>   2 *cups globe artichoke hearts (fresh,*
>   *frozen, or drained canned)*
>   2 *tablespoons butter or margarine*
>   1 *cup milk*
>   2 *cups water*
>   1 *teaspoon salt*
>   ⅛ *teaspoon white pepper*
>   1 *clove garlic, peeled and speared with*
>   *a toothpick*
>   ½ *cup beef consommé*
>   1 *teaspoon minced parsley*

If artichokes are fresh, parboil 20–25 minutes and drain. If frozen,
thaw just enough to separate. Quarter hearts, then slice thin cross-
wise. Stir-fry in butter in a saucepan (not aluminum) over moderately low heat 5 minutes; do not brown. Add all but last 2 ingredients, cover, and simmer over lowest heat 20 minutes. Discard garlic,
purée about half the mixture in an electric blender at low speed or
put through a food mill; return to pan. Add consommé and heat to
serving temperature, stirring now and then. Serve hot sprinkled with
parsley. About 125 calories per serving.

VARIATION:

Cold Artichoke Soup: Slice artichokes but do not fry; omit butter.
Simmer as directed, then purée and proceed as above. About 80 calories per serving.

TURNIP SOUP

Makes 4 servings

>   ½ *pound turnips, peeled and cut in small*
>   *dice*
>   1 *small yellow onion, peeled and minced*
>   2 *cups chicken or beef broth*
>   2 *cups water*
>   1 *teaspoon salt*

2 teaspoons Worcestershire sauce
1 teaspoon soy sauce
1 teaspoon minced chives
1 tablespoon slivered pimiento

Simmer all ingredients except chives and pimiento in a covered saucepan over moderately low heat 20–25 minutes. Stir in chives and pimiento and serve. About 35 calories per serving.

VARIATIONS:

Rutabaga Soup: Prepare as directed, substituting 2 cups diced, peeled rutabaga for turnip and increasing cooking time slightly, about 5–10 minutes. Same calories as turnip soup.

Parsnip Soup: Substitute 2 cups diced, peeled parsnips for turnips and proceed as recipe directs. Good with a little grated Parmesan sprinkled on top. About 70 calories per serving.

COCKALEEKIE

This old Scottish cock and leek soup used to be rich as a stew. Today you're more apt to be served the following version—with or without prunes.
Makes 4 servings

1 pound leeks, washed, trimmed, halved
lengthwise, and sliced ⅛" thick
(include some green tops)
1 tablespoon butter or margarine
1 quart chicken broth
½ teaspoon salt
⅛ teaspoon pepper
½ cup diced, cooked chicken meat
4–6 whole or coarsely chopped pitted
prunes (optional)
1 teaspoon minced parsley

Stir-fry leeks in butter in a saucepan over moderately low heat 2–3 minutes. Add all remaining ingredients except parsley, cover, and simmer 10 minutes. Sprinkle with parsley and serve. About 100 calories per serving without the optional prunes, 132 calories per serving with the prunes.

67

AVGOLEMONO SOUP
(Greek Chicken-Lemon Soup)

Makes 4 servings

> *1 quart chicken broth*
> *¼ cup uncooked rice*
> *Pinch mace or nutmeg*
> *3 egg yolks*
> *Juice of 1 lemon*
> *Salt*
> *Pepper*

Place broth, rice, and mace in a large saucepan, cover, and simmer 25–30 minutes until rice is very tender. Beat yolks with lemon juice; spoon a little hot broth into egg mixture, return to pan, and heat over lowest heat 1–2 minutes, stirring constantly, until no taste of raw egg remains; do not boil. Taste for salt and pepper and season as needed. About 130 calories per serving.

BASIC FRUIT SOUP

Slavs and Scandinavians sometimes serve a hot or cold fruit soup before the main course; berries, cherries, and plums are the favored "soup fruits."

Makes 4 servings

> *1 pint berries, washed and stemmed*
> *(strawberries, raspberries, blueberries,*
> *boysenberries, blackberries, or*
> *gooseberries)*
> *1 pint water or a ½ and ½ mixture of*
> *water and dry white wine*
> *¼ cup sugar (about)*
> *2 teaspoons lemon juice*
> *1 tablespoon cornstarch blended with*
> *2 tablespoons cold water*
> *Heavy cream, sour cream, or buttermilk*
> *(optional topping)*

Simmer berries in water in a covered saucepan 10 minutes until mushy; put through a food mill or purée in an electric blender at low speed, then press through a fine sieve. Return purée to pan, add remaining ingredients, and heat to a boil, stirring. Taste for sugar and add more, if needed. Serve hot or cold, topped, if you like, with cream. From about 70–120 calories per serving if made with water only, 130–55 if made with water and wine (strawberries and gooseberries are the lowest in calories). Add 50 calories per serving for each tablespoon heavy cream topping used, 30 calories for each tablespoon sour cream, and 5 calories for each tablespoon buttermilk.

VARIATIONS:

Quick Berry Soup: Substitute 2 (10-ounce) packages thawed frozen berries or 1 (1-pound) undrained can berries for the fresh. Do not cook; purée and sieve, then add enough water to make 1 quart. Heat with sugar (just enough to taste), lemon juice, and cornstarch paste as directed. About 115–30 calories per serving, depending on kind of berries used.

Sweet-Sour Fruit Soup: Prepare as directed, increasing sugar to 5 tablespoons and adding, at the same time, 3 tablespoons red or white wine vinegar. About 10 calories more per serving than Basic Fruit Soup.

APPLE SOUP

Serve as a first course or light dessert.
Makes 4–6 servings

  1 pound greenings or other tart cooking apples,
    peeled, cored, and sliced thin
  3 cups water
  1 teaspoon grated lemon rind
  2 teaspoons lemon juice
  ½ cup sugar (about)
  ½ teaspoon cinnamon
  ¼ teaspoon nutmeg
  1 cup sour cream blended with ½ cup milk
    (optional)

Place all but last ingredient in a saucepan, cover, and simmer about 20 minutes until apples are mushy. Put through a food mill or purée in an electric blender at low speed; taste for sugar and add more if needed. Serve hot or cold with a little of the sour cream mixture drizzled on top, if you like. About 145 calories for each of 4 servings, 100 for each of 6 without optional sour cream topping. Add 25 calories per serving for each tablespoon of topping used.

Meats

TERIYAKI-STYLE TENDERLOIN

Makes 4 servings

> 1½ pounds beef tenderloin in 1 piece
>
> Marinade:
>
> ¾ cup Japanese soy sauce
> ¼ cup mirin, sake, or medium-dry sherry
> 1 tablespoon light brown sugar (only if sake
>   or sherry is used)
> 2 teaspoons finely grated fresh gingerroot or
>   1 tablespoon minced preserved ginger

Place tenderloin in a large bowl. Mix marinade ingredients, pour over meat, cover, and let stand at room temperature 1½–2 hours, turning meat several times. Remove meat from marinade and broil 4" from the heat about 15 minutes, turning every 3 minutes and basting with marinade. (*Note:* This cooking time is for a medium-rare *teriyaki*. If you like it rarer, reduce cooking time to about 10–12 minutes, if more well done, increase it to 17 minutes.) To serve, cut in thin slices and top with a little marinade. About 290 calories per serving.

VARIATION:

Teriyaki Hors d'Oeuvre: Cut tenderloin into ¾"–1" cubes and marinate as directed; drain, reserving marinade. Broil 4" from heat 1–2 minutes, turn, baste with marinade, and broil 1–2 minutes longer. Skewer with toothpicks or bamboo skewers. Or, if you have a hibachi, set out the raw marinated cubes, long metal skewers, or fondue forks and let everyone broil their own teriyaki. Makes about 6–8 servings. About 185 calories for each of 6 servings, 140 calories for each of 8 servings.

STEAK FLORENTINE

Makes 2–3 servings

> 1 porterhouse steak, cut 1½" thick
> 1 clove garlic, peeled and cut in thin
>   slivers
> ⅛ teaspoon pepper
> 1 tablespoon olive oil
> ½ teaspoon salt
> Lemon wedges

Rub each side of steak well with garlic, pepper, and oil and let stand at room temperature 2 hours. Heat a large, heavy griddle over moderately high heat about 1 minute and brown steak quickly on both sides. Reduce heat to moderately low and cook steak 10–12 minutes on a side for very rare, 12–14 for rare, 15–17 for medium, and 18–20 for well done. Season with salt and serve with lemon wedges. About 465 calories for each of 2 servings, 310 calories for each of 3 servings.

ECONOMY MEAT LOAF

Makes 6 servings

> 1½ pounds ground beef
> 1 cup rolled oats
> 2 teaspoons salt
> ¼ teaspoon pepper
> 1 teaspoon prepared spicy yellow
>   mustard
> 1 teaspoon prepared horseradish
> 1 large yellow onion, peeled and chopped
>   fine
> ¾ cup milk or skim milk
> ¼ cup cold water

Preheat oven to 350° F. Using your hands, mix all ingredients together thoroughly. Pack into an ungreased 9" × 5" × 3" loaf pan. Bake, uncovered, 1 hour. Loosen loaf from pan, drain off drippings (save for gravy), invert on a heated platter, and serve. About 225 calories per serving.

TAMALE PIE

Makes 6 servings

Crust:

1 quart water
2 teaspoons salt
1 cup yellow cornmeal

Filling:

1 medium-size yellow onion, peeled and
  coarsely chopped
½ sweet green pepper, cored, seeded, and
  coarsely chopped
1 tablespoon cooking oil or bacon
  drippings
1 pound lean ground beef
1 clove garlic, peeled and crushed
1 tablespoon chili powder
¾ teaspoon salt
¼ teaspoon oregano
Pinch pepper
1 (8-ounce) can tomato sauce

Topping:

2 tablespoons finely grated Parmesan
  cheese

Preheat oven to 350° F. Bring water and salt to a boil in a large saucepan, very gradually add cornmeal, beating constantly so it doesn't lump. Turn heat to low and continue cooking and stirring about 5 minutes until quite thick. Spread ⅔ of mush in the bottom of a buttered 9″ × 9″ × 2″ pan and set aside; keep rest warm. For the filling, stir-fry onion and green pepper in oil in a large skillet over moderate heat 8–10 minutes until onion is golden; mix in meat, garlic, chili powder, salt, oregano, and pepper and stir-fry 5 minutes longer, breaking up clumps of meat. Mix in tomato sauce and simmer, uncovered, about 5 minutes; spoon over mush in pan, top with remaining mush, spreading as evenly over all as possible. Sprinkle with Parmesan and bake, uncovered, 30 minutes. Let stand at room temperature 10 minutes, then cut into large squares and serve. About 275 calories per serving.

SAUTÉED CALF'S LIVER

Liver is best on the rare side—faintly pink with rosy juices. If over-cooked, it becomes tough and dry.

Makes 2 servings

> 2 tablespoons butter or margarine
> ¾ pound calf's liver, sliced ¼" thick
> Pinch nutmeg (optional)
> Pinch summer savory (optional)
> ¼ teaspoon salt
> ⅛ teaspoon pepper

Melt butter in a large, heavy skillet over moderately high heat, let it foam up, then subside. Add liver and brown 2–3 minutes per side for rare, 3–3½ for medium. Sprinkle both sides with seasonings and serve. About 280 calories per serving.

BOMBAY LAMB SHANKS

Makes 2 servings

> 2 small lamb shanks, each cracked into
>   3 pieces

Marinade:

> 1 medium-size yellow onion, peeled and
>   coarsely chopped
> ½ cup yogurt
> ½ teaspoon curry powder
> ¼ teaspoon garlic powder
> ½ teaspoon poppy seeds, crushed in a
>   mortar and pestle
> 1 teaspoon salt
> ¼ teaspoon pepper
> ¼ teaspoon ginger
> ¼ teaspoon cinnamon
> 1 tablespoon lemon juice

Place lamb shanks in a large, deep bowl. Blend marinade ingredients in an electric blender at high speed 1 minute, then pour over shanks. Cover and chill 3–4 hours, turning shanks 1 or 2 times. Prepare a moderately hot charcoal fire. Place each shank on a large square of heavy foil, top with ¼ cup marinade, and wrap tightly. Reserve remaining marinade. Lay shanks on grill, not too close together, and cook 3″ from coals 1¼–1½ hours, turning 3–4 times with tongs. Unwrap 1 shank and test for tenderness—meat should begin to separate from bone. If it doesn't, rewrap and cook a little longer. When tender, unwrap shanks and lay directly on grill. Broil 5–7 minutes, brushing occasionally with marinade and turning shanks so they brown evenly. About 250 calories per serving.

Poultry and Seafood

TURKEY TIMBALES

Makes 4 servings

1 cup milk
1 cup soft white bread crumbs
2 tablespoons butter or margarine
1 tablespoon finely grated yellow onion
1 chicken bouillon cube
½ teaspoon salt
⅛ teaspoon pepper
⅛ teaspoon sage
⅛ teaspoon thyme
2 eggs, lightly beaten
1 cup finely ground cooked turkey meat

Preheat oven to 325° F. Mix all but last 2 ingredients in a saucepan and bring to a boil, stirring constantly. Remove from heat. Stir a little hot mixture into eggs, then return to pan and mix well. Mix in turkey. Spoon into 4 well-buttered custard cups and set in a shallow baking pan; pour enough water into pan to come halfway up cups. Bake, uncovered, about 35 minutes until just set. Loosen edges of timbales and invert gently on a hot platter. About 285 calories per serving.

HOT CHICKEN OR TURKEY LOAF

Makes 8 servings

>   3 cups finely chopped cooked chicken or turkey meat
>   2 cups dry white bread crumbs
>   ½ cup minced celery
>   2 pimientos, drained and coarsely chopped
>   1½ teaspoons salt
>   ¼ teaspoon pepper
>   1 tablespoon finely grated yellow onion
>   1 tablespoon lemon juice
>   2 teaspoons Worcestershire sauce
>   1 tablespoon minced parsley
>   2 cups chicken broth
>   3 eggs, lightly beaten

Preheat oven to 350° F. Mix together all but last 2 ingredients. Stir broth into eggs, then pour over chicken mixture and mix well. Lightly pack mixture into a greased 9″ × 5″ × 3″ loaf pan, set in a large baking pan, and pour in enough boiling water to come about halfway up loaf pan. Bake, uncovered, about 1 hour until loaf begins to pull away from sides of pan. Lift loaf pan from water bath and cool upright 5–10 minutes; loosen loaf, invert on a hot platter and ease out. Serve hot with chicken or mushroom gravy. Good cold, sliced thin and accompanied by salad. About 200 calories per serving if made with chicken (without gravy), 220 calories per serving if made with turkey.

VARIATIONS:

Surprise Chicken Loaf: Prepare chicken mixture as directed and pack half into loaf pan. Arrange 3 peeled hard-cooked eggs lengthwise down center of mixture, place rows of pimiento, stuffed green or pitted ripe olives on either side of eggs, cover with remaining chicken mixture and bake as directed. About 245 calories per serving.

Chicken and Rice Loaf: Prepare chicken mixture as directed but reduce bread crumbs to 1½ cups and add 1½ cups boiled rice. About 210 calories per serving.

75

CHICKEN CHOW MEIN

Makes 6 servings

½ pound mushrooms, wiped clean and sliced thin
6 scallions, minced (include some tops)
2 small sweet green peppers, cored, seeded,
    and minced
4 stalks celery, minced
2 tablespoons cooking oil
2½ cups chicken broth
2 tablespoons soy sauce
¼ cup cornstarch blended with ¼ cup cold water
½ teaspoon salt
⅛ teaspoon pepper
3 cups bite-size pieces cooked chicken meat,
    preferably white meat
1 (1-pound) can bean sprouts, drained
1 (3-ounce) can water chestnuts, drained
    and sliced thin

Stir-fry mushrooms, scallions, green peppers, and celery in oil in a large, heavy skillet over moderately high heat 8–10 minutes until golden brown. Add broth and soy sauce, turn heat to low, cover, and simmer 10 minutes. Mix in cornstarch paste, salt, and pepper and heat, stirring constantly, until thickened and clear. Add chicken, bean sprouts, and water chestnuts and heat and stir about 5 minutes, just to heat through. Taste for salt and adjust if needed. Serve over boiled rice. About 255 calories per serving (without rice).

MOO GOO GAI PEEN
(Chicken with Mushrooms)

Makes 2 servings

Breast of 1 large broiler-fryer, boned, halved,
    and skinned
2 tablespoons peanut oil
½ cup thinly sliced mushrooms
1 cup finely shredded Chinese cabbage
⅓ cup thinly sliced bamboo shoots
2 (½″) cubes fresh gingerroot, peeled and crushed

⅓ cup chicken broth
1 tablespoon dry sherry (optional)
½ (7-ounce) package frozen snow pea pods,
 slightly thawed
3 water chestnuts, sliced thin
2 teaspoons cornstarch blended with 1
 tablespoon cold water
¾ teaspoon salt (about)
⅛ teaspoon sugar

Cut chicken across the grain into strips about 2" long and ¼" wide; set aside. Heat 1 tablespoon oil in a large, heavy skillet over moderately high heat about 1 minute, add mushrooms, cabbage, bamboo shoots, and ginger, and stir-fry 2 minutes. Add broth, cover, and simmer 2–3 minutes. Pour all into a bowl and set aside. Wipe out skillet, heat remaining oil, and stir-fry chicken 2–3 minutes; if you like sprinkle with sherry and stir a few seconds longer. Return vegetables and broth to skillet, add snow peas and chestnuts, and heat, stirring until bubbling. Mix in cornstarch paste, salt, and sugar and heat, stirring until clear and slightly thickened; taste for salt and adjust as needed. Serve with boiled rice. About 250 calories per serving (without sherry or rice).

BRUNSWICK STEW

American Indian women, who invented Brunswick Stew, used to make it with squirrel or rabbit. If you have a hunter in the family, try it their way.
Makes 12–15 servings

1 (6-pound) stewing hen or capon,
 cleaned and dressed
1 gallon cold water
2 stalks celery (include tops)
1 tablespoon sugar
5 medium-size potatoes, peeled and cut in ½" cubes
3 medium-size yellow onions, peeled and
 coarsely chopped
6 large ripe tomatoes, peeled, cored, seeded, and
 coarsely chopped

2 (*10-ounce*) *packages frozen baby lima beans*
(*do not thaw*)
2 (*10-ounce*) *packages frozen whole kernel corn*
(*do not thaw*)
1 *medium-size sweet green pepper, cored and*
cut in short, thin slivers
2 *tablespoons salt* (*about*)
¼ *teaspoon pepper*

Remove fat from body cavity of bird, then place bird and giblets in a very large kettle. Add water and celery, cover, and simmer 1–2 hours until *just* tender. Remove bird and giblets from broth and cool. Strain broth and skim off fat. Rinse kettle, pour in broth, add sugar, all vegetables but corn and green pepper, cover, and simmer 1 hour. Meanwhile, skin chicken, cut meat in 1″ chunks and dice giblets. Return chicken and giblets to kettle, add remaining ingredients, cover, and simmer 40–45 minutes, stirring occasionally. Taste for salt, adding more if needed. Serve piping hot in soup bowls as a main dish. Particularly good with coleslaw and hushpuppies or crisp corn sticks. (*Note:* This stew freezes well.) About 310 calories for each of 12 servings, about 250 calories for each of 15 servings.

FILLETS OF FLOUNDER
EN PAPILLOTE

Makes 4 servings

4 *large flounder fillets* (*about 1½ pounds*)
1½ *teaspoons salt*
½ *cup minced scallions*
1 *tablespoon butter or margarine*
1 *tablespoon flour*
2 *ripe tomatoes, peeled, cored, seeded,*
and chopped fine
1 *teaspoon red or white wine vinegar*
½ *teaspoon basil or oregano*
⅛ *teaspoon pepper*

Preheat oven to 350° F. Cut 4 large squares of cooking parchment (available at gourmet shops) or heavy duty foil (large enough to wrap fillets); lay a fillet on each and sprinkle with 1 teaspoon salt. Sauté scallions in butter in a small skillet over moderate heat 3–5 minutes until limp; sprinkle in flour, add remaining salt and all other ingredients, and heat, stirring, over low heat 3–5 minutes to blend flavors. Spoon a little sauce over each fillet and wrap tightly drugstore style. Place packages on a baking sheet and bake 30–40 minutes; unwrap 1 package and check to see if fish flakes; if not, rewrap and bake a little longer. Serve in foil to retain all juices. About 180 calories per serving.

TUNA NIÇOISE

A cooling summer luncheon entree made with tuna, ripe olives, and tomatoes.
Makes 6 servings

> 2 (7-ounce) cans white meat tuna,
>   drained and flaked
> 1 yellow onion, peeled and chopped fine
> ½ clove garlic, peeled and crushed
> 2 tablespoons capers
> ¼ cup coarsely chopped ripe olives
> 1 stalk celery, chopped fine
> 1 tablespoon minced parsley
> 1 tablespoon minced fresh basil or
>   tarragon or ½ teaspoon of the dried
> 1 tablespoon minced fresh chives
> 3 tablespoons olive oil
> ⅓ cup mayonnaise
> ⅛ teaspoon pepper
> 6 large, crisped lettuce cups or 6 large
>   ripe tomatoes, hollowed out

Mix together all ingredients except lettuce cups or tomatoes, cover, and chill several hours. Mound into lettuce cups or tomatoes and serve. About 260 calories per serving if served in lettuce cups, 290 calories per serving if served in tomatoes.

SEAFOOD PROVENÇAL

Makes 6 servings

>2 *pounds fillets or steaks of delicate white fish*
>   *(cod, haddock, flounder, fluke, halibut, etc.)*
>1½ *teaspoons salt*
>¼ *teaspoon pepper*
>1 *clove garlic, peeled and crushed*
>1 *cup fish stock*
>3 *firm tomatoes, halved but not peeled*
>2 *tablespoons olive or other cooking oil*
>⅛ *teaspoon thyme*
>½ *cup soft white bread crumbs*
>2 *tablespoons melted butter or margarine*

Preheat oven to 350° F. Fold fillets envelope fashion, ends toward center, and arrange in a single layer in a well-buttered shallow 2½-quart casserole. Sprinkle with 1 teaspoon salt and ⅛ teaspoon pepper. Stir garlic into stock and pour over fish. Bake uncovered, basting 2 or 3 times, 20–30 minutes until fish will flake. Meanwhile, sauté tomatoes in oil in a skillet over moderate heat 4–5 minutes until lightly browned; keep warm. When fish is done, draw liquid off with a bulb baster. Arrange tomatoes around fish, sprinkle with thyme and remaining salt and pepper. Top with crumbs, drizzle with butter, and broil 3″–4″ from heat 1–2 minutes to brown. About 210 calories per serving.

Vegetables

ITALIAN-STYLE MARINATED ARTICHOKE HEARTS

Makes 4–6 servings

> ½ *cup low-calorie Italian dressing*
> 1 *clove garlic, peeled and crushed*
> *Juice of* ½ *lemon*
> *Pinch pepper*
> 2 *(9-ounce) packages frozen artichoke hearts,*
> *boiled and drained*

Mix dressing, garlic, lemon juice, and pepper and pour over artichoke hearts. Cover and marinate in the refrigerator 2–3 hours,
turning hearts occasionally. Toss well and serve cold as a vegetable
or salad. About 75 calories for each of 4 servings, 50 calories for
each of 6.

GREEN BEANS IN MUSTARD SAUCE

Makes 4 servings

> 1 *pound green beans, boiled and drained*
> *(reserve cooking water)*
> 1 *tablespoon butter or margarine*
> 1 *tablespoon flour*
> *Green bean cooking water plus enough*
> *milk to total* ¾ *cup*
> 3 *tablespoons prepared mild yellow mustard*
> 1 *tablespoon Worcestershire sauce*
> ½ *teaspoon salt*
> ¼ *teaspoon cayenne pepper*

Keep beans warm. Melt butter over moderate heat and blend in
flour. Add the ¾ cup liquid and heat, stirring constantly, until thick-

ened. Mix in remaining ingredients and heat, stirring, 2–3 minutes to blend flavors. Pour sauce over beans, toss lightly to mix, and serve. About 75 calories per serving.

BROCCOLI IN WHITE WINE SAUCE

Makes 4 servings

> 2 tablespoons butter or margarine
> ¼ cup dry white wine
> 1 (2-pound) head broccoli, parboiled and drained
> ¼ teaspoon salt
> ⅛ teaspoon pepper
> Pinch nutmeg

Add butter and wine to broccoli, cover, and simmer 5 minutes over low heat. Uncover and simmer 5–10 minutes longer, basting with pan liquid, until tender. Season with salt, pepper, and nutmeg and serve. About 115 calories per serving.

CANTONESE CARROTS WITH
GREEN PEPPER AND CELERY

Makes 4 servings

> 12–14 small young carrots, peeled
> 3 stalks celery
> ½ medium-size sweet green pepper,
>   cored and seeded
> 2 tablespoons peanut or other cooking oil
> 1 scallion, chopped fine (include tops)
> ¾ teaspoon salt

Cut carrots on the bias into diagonal slices about ¼″ thick. Cut celery the same way, making slices ⅛″ thick. Cut green pepper into matchstick strips. Heat oil in a large, heavy skillet over moderately low heat 1 minute. Add carrots and celery and stir-fry 4 minutes. Add green pepper and scallion and stir-fry 5 minutes or until carrots are crisp tender. Sprinkle vegetables with salt, toss, and serve. About 105 calories per serving.

STEWED TOMATOES

Makes 4 servings

> 4 large ripe tomatoes, peeled, cored, and quartered, or
>   1½ pounds Italian plum tomatoes, peeled
> 1 tablespoon water (optional)
> ¾ teaspoon salt
> ¼ teaspoon sugar
> Pinch pepper

Place tomatoes in a heavy saucepan, add water (if they seem dry) and remaining ingredients. Cover and simmer 5–7 minutes until *just* soft; uncover and simmer ½ minute longer. Serve in small bowls as a vegetable. About 35 calories per serving.

VARIATION:

Stewed Vegetables: Just before serving, stir in any of the following: 1 cup hot cooked whole kernel corn; 1 cup sautéed sliced mushrooms; 1½ cups hot cooked green beans; 2 cups hot cooked baby okra pods. Recipe too flexible for a meaningful calorie count.

Salads and Salad Dressings

WILTED CUCUMBERS

Makes 4 servings

> 2 medium-size cucumbers, peeled or not
>   (as you like) and sliced paper thin
> 1½ teaspoons salt
> 2 tablespoons boiling water
> 2 tablespoons sugar
> ⅓ cup white, tarragon, or cider vinegar
> Grinding of pepper

Layer cucumbers in a bowl, salting as you go, weight down, cover, and let stand at room temperature 1–2 hours. Drain, wash in a colander under cold running water, then drain and press out as much liquid as possible; pat dry on paper toweling. Mix water and sugar until sugar dissolves, add vinegar, pour over cucumbers, and toss well. Cover and chill 1–2 hours, mixing now and then. Top with a grinding of pepper and serve as is or in lettuce cups. About 40 calories per serving.

PERFECTION SALAD

Makes 6 servings

> 1 envelope unflavored gelatin
> ¼ cup sugar
> 1¼ cups water
> 2 tablespoons lemon juice
> 1 tablespoon cider vinegar
> ¾ teaspoon salt
> 1½ cups finely shredded green, red, or
>   Chinese cabbage or ½ cup of each
> ½ cup diced celery
> ¼ cup coarsely chopped pimiento-stuffed green olives
> ¼ cup minced sweet red or green pepper
> 2 tablespoons finely grated carrot

Sprinkle gelatin and sugar over water and heat, stirring, over moderately low heat until dissolved. Off heat, stir in lemon juice, vinegar, and salt; chill until syrupy. Fold in remaining ingredients, spoon into an ungreased 1-quart mold, and chill until firm. Unmold on lettuce leaves and serve with mayonnaise. About 55 calories per serving (without mayonnaise).

RAW ZUCCHINI SALAD

Makes 4–6 servings

> 2 cups thinly sliced unpeeled baby
>   zucchini, chilled
> 2 medium-size firm-ripe tomatoes, cored
>   and thinly sliced
> 1 medium-size red onion, peeled, sliced
>   paper thin, and separated into rings
> ¾ cup thinly sliced raw, peeled
>   mushrooms (optional)
> ⅓ cup French dressing
> 2 cups prepared mixed salad greens

Mix all ingredients except greens, cover, and chill 1 hour, turning now and then. Line a salad bowl with the greens, mound zucchini mixture on top, and toss at the table (there should be enough dressing for the greens, too; if not add a little more). About 185 calories for each of 4 servings, 125 calories for each of 6 servings.

TANGY LOW-CALORIE SALAD DRESSING

Good with any green salad.
Makes 1½ cups

> 1 tablespoon cornstarch
> 1 cup cold water
> 3 tablespoons salad oil
> ¼ cup cider vinegar
> 1 teaspoon salt
> 1 teaspoon sugar
> 2 tablespoons ketchup
> 1 teaspoon prepared mild yellow mustard
> ½ teaspoon paprika
> ½ teaspoon prepared horseradish
> ½ teaspoon Worcestershire sauce
> ½ teaspoon oregano

Blend cornstarch and water and heat and stir over moderate heat until thickened and clear. Off heat, beat in remaining ingredients with a rotary beater or electric mixer. Cover and chill well. Shake before using. About 20 calories per tablespoon.

MUSTARD SALAD DRESSING

Makes about 1½ cups

> 2 tablespoons butter or margarine
> 2 tablespoons flour
> 1 cup milk
> 1 teaspoon salt
> 1½ teaspoons sugar
> 2 teaspoons powdered mustard blended
>   with 2 tablespoons cold water
> ⅓ cup cider vinegar

Melt butter in a small saucepan over moderately low heat, blend in flour, add milk slowly, and cook and stir until thickened and smooth. Mix in salt, sugar, and mustard paste. Add vinegar, 1 tablespoon at a time, beating well after each addition. Cool dressing, then cover and chill 2–3 hours. Beat well before using. Use to dress any cooked vegetable or seafood salad. (*Note:* Dressing keeps well about a week in refrigerator.) About 20 calories per tablespoon.

Extra-Low-Calorie Mustard Dressing: Prepare as directed but use skim milk instead of regular. About 15 calories per tablespoon.

BUTTERMILK DRESSING

Dieters, note just *how* low the calories are.
Makes about 1½ cups

> ½ *cup cider vinegar*
> 1 *tablespoon salad oil*
> 1 *teaspoon salt*
> ⅛ *teaspoon white pepper*
> 1 *cup buttermilk*

Shake all ingredients in a jar with a tight-fitting lid and use to dress cabbage or crisp green salads. (*Note:* Dressing will keep about a week in the refrigerator.) About 10 calories per tablespoon.

À LA GRECQUE MARINADE

Leeks, zucchini, and certain other cooked vegetables are delicious when marinated in this delicate lemon and oil dressing. They may be served as a first course, a salad, or a vegetable.
Makes about 3 cups

> ⅓ *cup lemon juice*
> ½ *cup olive oil*
> 1 *pint hot water*
> ½ *teaspoon salt*
> ⅛ *teaspoon each fennel and coriander seeds*
> *tied in cheesecloth*
> 1 *bay leaf*
> 1 *(4″) sprig fresh thyme or* ⅛ *teaspoon dried thyme*
> *Pinch white pepper*

Mix all ingredients together and use in preparing vegetables that are to be served *à la grecque.* About 20 calories per tablespoon.

Desserts

GINGERED HONEYDEW MELON

Makes 4–6 servings

> 1 medium-size ripe honeydew melon
> (about 3½–4 pounds)
> 1½ cups water
> ½ cup sugar
> 6 (1-inch) squares crystallized ginger
> ½ lemon, quartered

Halve melon lengthwise and scoop out seeds; remove rind and cut melon in bite-size cubes; place in a large mixing bowl. Simmer water, uncovered, with sugar and ginger about 30 minutes, stirring occasionally. Off heat, add lemon and cool to lukewarm. Pour syrup and lemon over melon, toss to mix, cover, and chill 3–4 hours. Remove lemon, spoon melon into stemmed goblets, and top with a little of the syrup. About 65 calories for each of 6 servings, 100 for each of 4.

GREEN GRAPES AND SOUR CREAM

One of the easiest elegant desserts.
Makes 4 servings

> 3 cups seedless green grapes, stemmed,
> washed, dried, and chilled
> ½ cup sour cream or unflavored yogurt
> ¼ cup dark brown sugar

Mix grapes and sour cream, spoon into dessert bowls, sprinkle with sugar, and serve. About 135 calories per serving if made with yogurt.

STRAWBERRIES GRAND MARNIER

Dieters won't feel deprived if served this dessert.
Makes 4 servings

> 1 quart fresh strawberries, washed,
> stemmed, and halved lengthwise
> 2–3 tablespoons superfine sugar (optional)
> ⅓ cup Grand Marnier

Taste berries and, if too tart, sprinkle with sugar. Let stand 10 minutes at room temperature, then toss lightly to mix. Pour Grand Marnier over berries and toss again; cover and chill several hours, turning berries occasionally. Serve topped with some of the Grand
Marnier and, if you like, sprigged with mint. About 100 calories per
serving (without sugar).

LEMON OR LIME GRANITÉ

Granité is a granular ice frozen without being stirred. It can be
served at the mush stage or frozen hard, then scraped up in fine,
feathery shavings. Particularly good topped with a little fruit liqueur
or rum.
Makes about 1½ quarts

> 1 quart water
> 2 cups sugar
> 1 cup lemon or lime juice
> 1 tablespoon finely grated lemon or lime
> rind

Bring water and sugar to a boil in a saucepan, stirring, then reduce
heat and simmer, uncovered, 5 minutes. Cool, mix in juice and rind.
Pour into 3 refrigerator trays, cover, and freeze to a mush without
stirring. Spoon into goblets and serve or freeze hard, scrape up with a
spoon, and pile into goblets. About 130 calories per ½-cup serving.

VARIATIONS:

Orange Granité: Prepare as directed, substituting 1 quart orange
juice for the water, reducing sugar to ¾ cup and lemon juice to 2 tablespoons; also use orange rind instead of lemon. About 85 calories
per ½-cup serving.

Fruit Granité: Boil 3 cups water and 1½ cups sugar into syrup as directed. Cool, add 2 tablespoons lemon juice and 2 cups puréed fruit (any berries, peaches, pineapple, sweet cherries); omit rind. Freeze and serve as directed. About 140–50 calories per ½-cup serving depending upon fruit used.

Coffee or Tea Granité: Boil 1 cup each water and sugar into syrup as directed; cool, add 3 cups strong black coffee or tea and to tea mixture, add ¼ cup lemon juice. Freeze and serve as directed. About 65 calories per ½-cup serving.

Melon Granité: Mix 1 quart puréed ripe melon (any kind) with ½–1 cup sugar (depending on sweetness of melon) and 2 tablespoons lemon juice; let stand 1 hour at room temperature, stirring now and then, until sugar is dissolved. Freeze as directed. About 65 calories per ½-cup serving *if* made with ½ cup sugar, 135 calories if made with 1 cup sugar.

GINGERED ORANGE FLUFF

Makes 4 servings

> 1 cup boiling water
> 1 envelope low-calorie orange-flavored gelatin
>   (*there are 2 envelopes in a ¾-ounce package*)
> ½ cup orange or tangerine juice
> ½ cup low-calorie ginger ale
> Pinch ginger

Mix boiling water and gelatin dessert until dissolved; stir in remaining ingredients. Chill until mixture mounds when dropped from a spoon, then beat with a rotary beater until foamy. Spoon into serving dishes and chill until firm. Serve cold. About 25 calories per serving.

VARIATIONS:
Substitute any other flavor of low-calorie fruit gelatin for the orange, mixing with an appropriate fruit juice: apple and apple juice (26 calories per serving), peach and peach nectar (26 calories per serving), raspberry or strawberry and cranberry juice (30 calories per serving), grape and grape juice (31 calories per serving), pineapple and pineapple juice (28 calories per serving).

BAKED CUSTARD

Makes 10 servings

> 5 eggs (6 if you plan to bake custard in
> a single large dish)
> ⅔ cup sugar
> ¼ teaspoon salt
> 1 teaspoon vanilla
> 1 quart milk, scalded
> Nutmeg or mace

Preheat oven to 325° F. Beat eggs lightly with sugar, salt, and vanilla; gradually stir in hot milk. Pour into 10 custard cups or a 2-quart baking dish (buttered if you want to unmold custards). Sprinkle with nutmeg, set in a large shallow pan, and pour in warm water to a depth of 1″. Bake, uncovered, about 1 hour until a knife inserted midway between center and rim comes out clean. Remove custards from water bath and cool to room temperature. Chill slightly before serving. About 160 calories per serving. By making custard with skim milk, you can reduce calories to about 125 per serving.

VARIATION:

Vanilla Bean Custard: Prepare as directed, substituting a 2″ piece vanilla bean for the extract; heat bean in milk as it scalds; remove before mixing milk into eggs. About 160 calories per serving.

ANGEL FOOD CAKE

If you follow the directions exactly, you'll bake a tall and tender cake.
Makes a 10″ tube cake

> 1½ cups sifted sugar
> 1 cup sifted cake flour
> 1 teaspoon cream of tartar
> ¼ teaspoon salt
> 12 egg whites, at room temperature
> 1 teaspoon vanilla
> ½ teaspoon almond extract
> 1 teaspoon lemon juice

Preheat oven to 325° F. Sift ¾ cup sugar with the flour and set aside. Sprinkle cream of tartar and salt over egg whites; beat with a wire whisk or rotary beater until *very* soft peaks form (whites should *flow, not run,* when bowl is tipped). Sift a little of the remaining sugar over whites and gently fold in, using a whisk; repeat until all sugar is mixed in. Now sift a little sugar-flour mixture over whites, and fold in with the whisk; repeat until all is incorporated (it may take as many as 10 additions). Fold in vanilla, almond extract, and lemon juice. Pour batter into an *ungreased* 10″ tube pan and bake 1–1¼ hours until cake is lightly browned and has pulled from the sides of pan. Invert pan and cool cake thoroughly in pan; then loosen edges with a spatula and turn out. Leave plain or frost as desired. About 120 calories for a piece equal to ½12 of the cake (unfrosted).

POACHED MERINGUE RING

A beautiful base for sliced fresh berries or any dessert sauce.
Makes 6 servings

> *6 egg whites*
> *⅛ teaspoon cream of tartar*
> *¼ teaspoon salt*
> *¾ cup superfine sugar*
> *1 teaspoon vanilla*
> *1 teaspoon lemon juice*
> *¼ teaspoon almond extract*

Preheat oven to 325° F. Beat egg whites, cream of tartar, and salt with a rotary egg beater until foamy. Add sugar, a little at a time, beating well after each addition. Continue to beat until whites stand in stiff peaks. Fold in vanilla, lemon juice, and almond extract. Pack mixture in an ungreased 6-cup ring mold. Set mold in a shallow pan of cold water and bake, uncovered, 1 hour until meringue is lightly browned and pulls from the sides of mold. Remove meringue from oven and water bath and let cool upright in mold to room temperature. Loosen edges carefully with a spatula and unmold by inverting on a dessert platter. Cut into wedges and serve as is or with a generous ladling of dessert sauce or with sliced fresh berries. About 110 calories per serving (without sauce or fruit).

DESSERT CARDINAL SAUCE

Use as a dessert sauce for ice cream, sherbet, or fresh fruit.
Makes about 5 cups

> 1 (10-ounce) package frozen raspberries, thawed
> ½ cup superfine sugar
> 1 tablespoon lemon juice
> 2–3 tablespoons kirsch (optional)
> 2 pints fresh strawberries, washed,
>   stemmed, and sliced thin

Purée raspberries in an electric blender at high speed or put through
a food mill, then strain. Add ¼ cup sugar, lemon juice, and, if you
like, the kirsch; stir well. Mix strawberries with remaining sugar.
Gently stir raspberry sauce into strawberries. About 10 calories per
tablespoon made without kirsch, 12 calories per tablespoon made
with kirsch.

LOW-CALORIE DESSERT TOPPING

Makes 4 servings

> 3 tablespoons ice water
> 3 tablespoons nonfat dry milk powder
> 2 teaspoons lemon juice
> Few drops liquid noncaloric sweetener
>   or 2 teaspoons low-calorie granulated
>   sugar substitute
> ¼ teaspoon vanilla or almond extract

Pour ice water into a chilled bowl, sprinkle powdered milk on surface, and beat with a rotary or electric beater until soft peaks form.
Add lemon juice, sweeten to taste, add vanilla, and beat until stiff
peaks form. Use at once. About 14 calories per serving.

VARIATION:

Low-Calorie Orange Dessert Topping: Substitute 1 tablespoon frozen, slightly thawed orange juice concentrate diluted with 2 tablespoons ice water for the ice water, omit vanilla, and after whipping
fold in 1 tablespoon finely grated orange rind. About 20 calories per
serving.

Calorie Counter /
Calories Burned per Hour

Here is an unusual approach to personal fitness. The Calorie Counter is not a counter of calories consumed at each meal, but a counter of calories burned per hour at various weights.

This chart was developed to help you learn to balance your caloric intake (eating) with your caloric outgo (activity)—the only healthful way of maintaining or losing weight.

For example, suppose you consume 2400 calories worth of food during a 24-hour period, and your level of activity is such that you burn off exactly 2400 calories as you work, sleep and play your way through the day. Supply and demand are equal. Your body neither calls on reserves to make up a deficit, nor does it deposit extra calories in the form of fat. You're maintaining your weight.

But, if you take in 2400 calories and burn off only 2300 calories of them, your body will "store" those 100 unnecessary calories in its fat cells until such time they're needed for energy.

One pound of fat is the equivalent of 3500 unnecessary calories. (Whether these calories were ingested in the form of sirloin steak, ice cream or raw carrots makes no difference. A calorie is a calorie is a calorie.) With this in mind, you can see that if you eat 100 calories more than you burn off through physical activity, at the end of 35 days you'll have gained a pound. And if you continue on at the same rate, you'll be 10 pounds heavier at the end of the year.

Most overweight problems are the result of being just a few calories per day out of balance. This chart shows you which kind of activities burn the most calories to assist you in getting your weight under control.

Many researchers are convinced that only through exercise can you properly control your weight without dangerously affecting the nutrients you need for healthful living. While it is true that you must burn 3500 calories to lose 1 pound of fat, you must remember that walking 20 minutes a day will burn up approximately 100 additional calories per day. In a year's time that is 10 pounds—pounds lost forever.

Activity:	Calories Burned Per Hour:		
	99 pounds	125 pounds	152 pounds
Badminton or Volleyball	225	285	345
Baseball	185	234	284
Basketball	278	352	426
Bicycling, on level, 5.5 mph.	198	251	304
13 mph.	424	537	651
Bowling	263	333	404
Calisthenics	198	251	304
Dancing, moderate	165	209	253
Dressing or Showering	126	160	193
Driving	118	150	181
Eating	55	70	85
Gardening	140	178	215
Golf	214	271	328
Hill Climbing	386	488	591
Horseback Riding, trot	267	338	409
Housework	161	203	246
Office Work	118	150	181
Mowing Grass	176	222	269
Ping-Pong	153	194	235
Running, 7 mph.	552	699	847
9 mph.	757	959	1161
in place, 140 counts/min.	964	1222	1479
Sailing	118	150	181
Shoveling Snow	307	389	471
Skating, moderate	225	285	345
Skiing, downhill	382	483	585
level, 5 mph.	463	586	709
Sleeping	46	59	71
Swimming, crawl, 45 yds./min.	345	437	529
Tennis, moderate	274	347	420
vigorous	386	488	591
Walking, 2 mph.	139	176	213
4½ mph.	261	331	401
Watching Television	47	60	72
Water Skiing	307	391	473

Vitamin Counter

Counting calories or carbohydrates, invigorating daily activities and a planned exercise program—all these are important to your general well-being, to help keep you slim and trim, healthy and happy.

But there is another aspect to maintaining a healthy body that is often overlooked or forgotten: The importance of vitamins. Herewith, a Vitamin Counter to keep nutritional tabs on your food intake, whether dieting or not, whether thick or thin. First, some background on vitamins:

VITAMINS IN OUR FOOD

We eat in order to live, and, to live right, we must eat right; we must eat enough of the foods that contain certain substances vital to our health. Vitamins are one group of these vital substances. If we don't get sufficient vitamin supplies, our skins can grow dry and scaly, our gums can bleed, our eyes can burn, our hair can fall out, and we can suffer from headaches, indigestion, and a variety of other ailments. Plants and most animals manufacture vitamins right in their own bodies. Since human beings can't do that, we have to get our vitamins from outside sources. And the natural source for our supply of vitamins is our food. Most experts agree that all the vitamins we need are contained in the foods we eat—or the foods we *should* be eating. But what are the foods that contain the vitamins we seek? And in what quantity can these vitamins be found?

On the following pages, you'll find over 1000 alphabetical listings of popular foods/beverages in common household measures and their vitamin content. We have included *Vitamin A, Thiamine, Riboflavin, Niacin* and *Vitamin C,* those considered to be the "major vitamins." Below is a brief description of each of these vitamins, and their MDR (Minimum Daily Requirement) suggested for adults by the Food and Nutrition Board of the National Research Council.

VITAMIN A (*Carotene*) is necessary for good vision; proper tooth development; health of the membranes lining the mouth and the digestive, respiratory and genito-urinary tracts; and resistance to infection. Deficiencies can cause night blindness, dry skin and hair, gastrointestinal disorders and sterility. Extreme deficiencies can lead to total blindness. MDR is 4000 I.U. for women.

THIAMINE (*Vitamin B₁*) is needed to help break down the sugar in the tissues in order to supply energy. It also helps regulate the nerve processes and the digestive tract. Deficiencies can cause tiredness, loss of appetite, abnormalities in the heart rhythm and personality disorders like moodiness and depression. In extreme cases, the disease called *beriberi* can develop. MDR is 1.2 mg. for women.

RIBOFLAVIN (*Vitamin B₂*) furthers general growth. It is necessary to metabolize protein in the body and help the body assimilate iron. The proper functioning of the gastrointestinal tract depends on it. Deficiencies can cause cracks at the corner of the mouth, dermatitis, baldness, premature wrinkles, split fingernails, general weakness and nerve disorders. MDR is 1.2 mg. for women.

NIACIN (*Nicotinic Acid*), which is one of the B complex of vitamins, also is needed to break down sugar in the tissues. It helps prevent migraine headaches and improves the circulation. Lack of it can produce scaly skin, dermatitis, inflammation of the mucous membranes, diarrhea and psychic changes. Extreme deficiencies can lead to the disease called *pellagra,* which produces painful disorders of the skin and digestive system. MDR is 13.0 mg. for women.

VITAMIN C (*Ascorbic Acid*) raises resistance to infection, furthers tooth and bone development, helps regulate the heart and strengthens the blood vessels and circulatory system. Lack of it can result in sore gums, excessive bleeding and bruising, slow healing, general debility, and, in extreme instances, *scurvy,* a degenerative disease of the skin and connective tissues. MDR is 45 mg. for women.

Other vitamins considered to be of importance in human nutrition include Vitamin D, Vitamin E and the rest of the B-complex vitamins:

VITAMIN D promotes the absorption of calcium and phosphorous from the digestive tract. Extreme deficiencies can lead to *rickets,* a softening of the bones, in children. The National Food Council makes no specific recommendations for the amount of Vitamin D needed by the adult, but the commonly suggested MDR is 400 I.U. per day. The best source of Vitamin D is sunlight. Foods which contain it are liver, egg yolk, saltwater fish and fish-liver oil.

VITAMIN E protects the red blood corpuscles and is said to have beneficial effects on the heart, circulatory and reproductive systems, and many other bodily parts and processes (but this has not yet been proven to everyone's satisfaction). Vitamin E is widely distributed in foods. Among its richest sources are vegetables and vegetable oils, milk, whole-grain (unrefined) cereals, soybeans, seeds, nuts, meat and eggs. No MDR has been suggested by the National Research Council, because it feels that everyone gets sufficient quantities in even the most barely adequate diets; however, 12 or 15 I.U. are generally recommended.

OTHER B VITAMINS, besides thiamine, riboflavin and niacin, include *pyridoxine (Vitamin B₆), cobalamin (Vitamin B₁₂), pantothenic acid* and *folic acid.* These are necessary for proper functioning of many body processes. No MDR has been established as deficiencies in these vitamins are rare. Good sources for them are liver, muscle meats, green leafy vegetables, whole-grain cereals and eggs. Most foods rich in other B vitamins are good sources for these, as well.

Abbreviations:

diam.	diameter
fl.	fluid
lb.	pound
I.U.	International Units
mg.	milligrams
n.a.	not available (lack of reliable data)
oz.	ounce
tbsp.	tablespoon
tr.	trace
tsp.	teaspoon
0	amount, if present, too small to be measured

FOOD AND MEASURE	Vit. A (I.U.)	Thia. (mg.)	Rib. (mg.)	Nia. (mg.)	Vit. C (mg.)
Acerola, fresh, 10 fruits (1″ diam.)	n.a.	.02	.05	.3	1066
Acerola juice, fresh, 1 cup	n.a.	.05	.15	1.0	3872
Almonds, dried, in shell, 1 lb.	0	.44	1.67	6.3	tr.
dried, 10 nuts	0	.02	.09	.4	tr.
dried, shelled, 1 lb.	0	1.09	4.17	15.9	tr.
dried, slivered, 1 cup	0	.28	1.06	4.0	tr.
dried, chopped, 1 tbsp.	0	.02	.07	.3	tr.
roasted in oil, salted, 1 lb.	0	.23	4.17	15.9	0
roasted in oil, salted, 1 cup (about 120 nuts)	0	.08	1.44	5.5	0
Amaranth leaves, raw, 1 lb.	27,670	.36	.73	6.4	363
Apple, fresh, with skin, 1 lb.	410	.14	.09	.5	18
fresh, with skin, 1 apple (3″ diam.)	150	.05	.03	.2	7
fresh, pared, 1 apple (3″ diam.)	60	.05	.03	.2	3
dried, rings, 8 oz.	n.a.	.14	.27	1.1	23
dried, rings, cooked, with/ without sugar, 1 cup	n.a.	.03	.08	.3	tr.
frozen, sliced, sweetened, 8 oz.	45	.03	.07	.5	16
Apple butter, 1 cup	0	.03	.06	.6	6
Apple juice, canned, 1 cup	n.a.	.02	.05	.2	2
Applesauce, canned, sweetened, 1 cup	100	.05	.03	.1	3
Applesauce, canned, unsweetened, 1 cup	100	.05	.02	.1	2
Apricot, fresh, 1 lb.	11,510	.13	.17	2.6	43
fresh, 3 apricots	2,890	.03	.04	.6	11
fresh, halves, 1 cup	4,190	.05	.06	.9	16
canned in syrup, halves, 1 cup with liquid	4,490	.05	.05	1.0	10
canned, water pack, halves, 1 cup with liquid	4,500	.05	.05	1.0	10
dehydrated nuggets, 8 oz.	31,980	tr.	.18	8.2	34
dehydrated nuggets, cooked, sweetened, 1 cup	8,400	tr.	.06	2.4	6
dried, halves, 8 oz.	24,720	.03	.37	7.5	27
dried, halves, 1 cup	14,170	.01	.21	4.3	16
dried, halves, 10 large halves	5,230	tr.	.08	1.6	6
dried, halves, cooked, sweetened, 1 cup	7,020	.01	.11	2.4	5

FOOD AND MEASURE	Vit. A (I.U.)	Thia. (mg.)	Rib. (mg.)	Nia. (mg.)	Vit. C (mg.)
dried, halves, cooked,					
unsweetened, 1 cup	7,500	.01	.13	2.5	8
frozen, sweetened, 8 oz.	3,810	.05	.09	1.8	64
Apricot nectar, canned, 1 cup	2,380	.03	.03	.5	8
Artichoke, globe, boiled, drained,					
1 bud (13½ oz.)	230	.11	.06	1.1	12
Asparagus, fresh, raw, 1 lb.	4,080	.82	.91	6.8	150
fresh, boiled, drained, 4 spears					
(½″ diam. base)	540	.10	.11	.8	16
fresh, boiled, drained, cuts, 1 cup	1,310	.23	.26	2.0	38
canned, spears, 1 cup with liquid	1,240	.15	.22	2.0	37
canned, cuts, 1 cup with liquid	1,220	.14	.22	1.9	36
canned, drained, 4 spears					
(½″ diam. base)	640	.05	.08	.6	12
canned, drained, cuts, 1 cup	1,880	.14	.24	1.9	35
frozen, boiled, drained, 4 spears					
(½″ diam. base)	470	.10	.08	.7	16
frozen, boiled, drained, cuts,					
1 cup	1,530	.25	.23	1.8	41
Avocado, California, ½ avocado					
(3⅛″ diam.)	310	.12	.22	1.7	15
Florida, ½ avocado					
(3⅝″ diam.)	440	.17	.31	2.4	21
cubes, 1 cup	440	.17	.30	2.4	21
mashed, 1 cup	670	.25	.46	3.7	32

B

FOOD AND MEASURE	Vit. A (I.U.)	Thia. (mg.)	Rib. (mg.)	Nia. (mg.)	Vit. C (mg.)
Bacon, cured, raw, 1 lb.	0	1.63	.50	8.2	n.a.
fried, drained, 2 thick slices					
(12 per lb. raw)	0	.12	.08	1.2	n.a.
fried, drained, 2 medium slices					
(20 per lb. raw)	0	.08	.05	.8	n.a.
Bacon, Canadian, unheated, 1 lb.	0	3.76	1.00	21.3	n.a.
Bacon, Canadian, fried, drained,					
1 slice (3⅜″ diam.)	0	.19	.04	1.1	n.a.
Baking powder, 1 tbsp.	0	0	0	0	0
Bamboo shoots, raw, 1″ cuts, 1 cup	30	.23	.11	.9	6
Banana, whole, 1 large (9¾″ long)	260	.07	.08	1.0	14
whole, 1 medium (8¾″ long)	230	.06	.07	.8	12
sliced, 1 cup	290	.08	.09	1.1	15

red, whole, 1 average (7¼" long)	520	.07	.05	.8	13
red, sliced, 1 cup	600	.08	.06	.9	15
plantain (baking type),					
1 average (11" long)	n.a.	.16	.11	1.6	37
Barbecue sauce, 1 cup	900	.03	.03	.8	13
Barley, pearled, light, 1 cup	0	.24	.10	6.2	0
Barley, pearled, pot or Scotch, 1 cup	0	.42	.14	7.4	0
Bass, smallmouth or largemouth,					
raw, 4 oz.	n.a.	.11	.03	2.4	n.a.
Beans, baked, canned, with					
tomato sauce, 1 cup	150	.18	.10	1.5	5
with frankfurters and tomato					
sauce, 1 cup	330	.18	.15	3.3	tr.
with pork and tomato sauce, 1 cup	330	.20	.08	1.5	5
with pork and molasses sauce,					
1 cup	n.a.	.15	.10	1.3	n.a.
Beans, green, raw, cuts, 1 lb.	2,720	.36	.50	2.3	86
boiled in small amount water,					
drained, 1 cup	680	.09	.11	.6	15
boiled in large amount water,					
drained, 1 cup	680	.08	.10	.4	13
canned, 1 cup with liquid	690	.07	.10	.7	10
canned, drained, 1 cup	630	.04	.07	.4	5
frozen, boiled, drained, cuts, 1 cup	780	.09	.12	.5	7
frozen, boiled, drained, French					
style, 1 cup	690	.08	.10	.4	9
Beans, Great Northern, dry, 1 cup	0	1.17	.40	4.3	n.a.
Beans, Great Northern, cooked,					
1 cup	0	.25	.13	1.3	0
Beans, lima, immature seeds,					
raw, 1 lb.	1,320	1.09	.54	6.4	132
boiled, drained, 1 cup	480	.31	.17	2.2	29
canned, 1 cup with liquid	320	.10	.10	1.2	17
canned, drained, 1 cup	320	.05	.09	.9	10
frozen, baby, boiled, drained,					
1 cup	400	.16	.09	2.2	22
frozen, Fordhook, boiled,					
drained, 1 cup	390	.12	.09	1.7	29
Beans, pea or navy, dry, 1 cup	0	1.33	.45	4.9	n.a.
Beans, pea or navy, cooked, 1 cup	0	.27	.13	1.3	0
Beans, red kidney, dry, 1 cup	40	.94	.37	4.3	n.a.
cooked, 1 cup	10	.20	.11	1.3	n.a.
canned, 1 cup with liquid	10	.13	.10	1.5	n.a.
Beans, yellow or wax, cuts,					
raw, 1 lb.	1,130	.36	.50	2.3	91

FOOD AND MEASURE	Vit. A (I.U.)	Thia. (mg.)	Rib. (mg.)	Nia. (mg.)	Vit. C (mg.)
boiled, drained, 1 cup	290	.09	.11	.6	16
canned, 1 cup with liquid	140	.07	.10	.7	12
canned, drained, 1 cup	140	.04	.07	.4	7
frozen, boiled, drained, 1 cup	140	.09	.11	.5	8
Bean sprouts, mung, uncooked, 1 cup	20	.14	.14	.8	20
Bean sprouts, mung, cooked, 1 cup	30	.11	.13	.9	8
Bean sprouts, soy, uncooked, 1 cup	80	.24	.21	.8	14
Bean sprouts, soy, cooked, 1 cup	100	.20	.19	.9	5
Beef, choice grade retail cuts, meat only:					
chuck, braised, lean with fat, 4 oz.	78	.05	.19	4.0	n.a.
chuck, braised, lean only, 4 oz.	28	.06	.25	5.1	n.a.
club steak, broiled, lean with fat, 4 oz.	80	.07	.19	4.9	n.a.
club steak, broiled, lean only, 4 oz.	25	.09	.26	6.6	n.a.
flank steak, braised, lean, 4 oz.	13	.06	.26	5.2	n.a.
ground beef, broiled, lean with 10% fat, 4 oz.	23	.11	.26	6.8	n.a.
ground beef, broiled, lean with 21% fat, 4 oz.	43	.10	.24	6.1	n.a.
porterhouse steak, broiled, lean with fat, 4 oz.	80	.07	.18	4.8	n.a.
porterhouse steak, broiled, lean only, 4 oz.	23	.09	.26	6.7	n.a.
rib, roasted, lean with fat, 4 oz.	92	.06	.17	4.1	n.a.
rib, roasted, lean only, 4 oz.	23	.08	.24	5.8	n.a.
round, broiled, lean and fat, 4 oz.	34	.09	.25	6.4	n.a.
round, broiled, lean only, 4 oz.	10	.09	.27	6.8	n.a.
rump, roasted, lean with fat, 4 oz.	57	.07	.21	4.9	n.a.
rump, roasted, lean only, 4 oz.	18	.08	.25	5.9	n.a.
sirloin, flat-bone, broiled, lean with fat, 4 oz.	68	.07	.21	5.2	n.a.
sirloin, flat-bone, broiled, lean only, 4 oz.	18	.09	.26	6.8	n.a.
sirloin, round-bone, broiled, lean with fat, 4 oz.	60	.07	.21	5.3	n.a.
sirloin, round-bone, broiled, lean only, 4 oz.	13	.10	.28	7.3	n.a.
T-bone steak, broiled, lean with fat, 4 oz.	85	.06	.18	4.7	n.a.

T-bone steak, broiled, lean only, 4 oz.	18	.09	.26	6.7	n.a.
Beef, corned, cooked, 4 oz.	n.a.	.02	.41	1.7	0
canned, 4 oz.	n.a.	.02	.27	3.8	0
hash, with potato, canned, 4 oz.	n.a.	.01	.10	2.4	n.a.
hash, with potato, canned, 1 cup	n.a.	.02	.20	4.6	n.a.
Beef, dried (chipped), 5-oz. jar	n.a.	.10	.45	5.4	0
Beef kidney, liver, tongue, see Kidney, Liver or Tongue					
Beef, potted, 1 cup	n.a.	.07	.50	2.7	n.a.
Beef pot pie, frozen, 8 oz.	1,860	.25	.27	4.6	7
Beef-vegetable stew, canned, 1 cup	2,380	.07	.12	2.5	7
Beer, 4.5% alcohol, 12-fl.-oz. can or bottle	n.a.	.01	.11	2.2	n.a.
Beets, peeled, raw, 1 lb.	90	.14	.23	1.8	45
boiled, drained, whole, 2 beets (2″ diam.)	20	.03	.04	.3	6
boiled, drained, diced or sliced, 1 cup	30	.05	.07	.5	10
canned, diced or sliced, 1 cup with liquid	20	.02	.05	.2	7
canned, drained, diced, sliced or whole, 1 cup	30	.02	.05	.2	5
Beet greens, leaves and stems, raw, 1 lb.	27,670	.45	1.00	1.8	136
Beet greens, boiled, drained, 1 cup	7,400	.10	.22	.4	22
Biscuit, mix, dry form, 1-cup packet	tr.	.53	.31	3.6	tr.
baked, made with milk, 1 biscuit (2″ diam. × 1¼″)	tr.	.08	.07	.6	tr.
Blackberries, fresh, 1 cup	290	.04	.06	.6	30
canned in syrup, 1 cup with liquid	330	.03	.05	.5	18
canned, water pack, 1 cup with liquid	340	.05	.05	.5	17
frozen, sweetened, 1 cup	200	.03	.14	.9	11
frozen, unsweetened, 1 cup	210	.03	.16	1.3	16
Blackberry juice, canned, unsweetened, 1 cup	n.a.	.05	.07	.7	25
Blackeye peas, see Cowpeas					
Blueberries, fresh, 1 cup	150	.04	.09	.7	20
Blueberries, frozen, sweetened, 1 cup	70	.09	.12	.9	18
Bluefish, raw, meat only, 4 oz.	n.a.	.14	.10	2.2	n.a.
Bluefish, broiled with butter, meat only, 4 oz.	50	.13	.11	2.2	n.a.
Bologna, sliced, 4 oz.	n.a.	.18	.25	2.9	n.a.

FOOD AND MEASURE	Vit. A (I.U.)	Thia. (mg.)	Rib. (mg.)	Nia. (mg.)	Vit. C (mg.)
Boysenberries, fresh, 1 cup	290	.04	.06	.6	30
canned, water pack, 1 cup with liquid	320	.02	.24	1.7	17
frozen, sweetened, 1 cup	200	.03	.14	.9	11
frozen, unsweetened, 1 cup	210	.03	.16	1.3	16
Braunschweiger, 4 oz.	7,410	.20	1.64	9.3	n.a.
Brazil nuts, in shell, 1 lb.	tr.	2.09	.26	3.5	n.a.
Brazil nuts, shelled, 1 lb.	tr.	4.35	.54	7.3	n.a.
Brazil nuts, shelled, 1 cup (about 32 large nuts)	tr.	1.34	.17	2.2	n.a.
Breads, commercial (enriched):					
Boston brown, canned, 1 slice (3¼″ diam. × ½″)	0	.05	.03	.5	0
cracked wheat, 1 slice (18 slices per 1 lb. loaf)	tr.	.03	.02	.3	tr.
French, 1 slice (5″ × 2½″ × 1″)	tr.	.10	.08	.9	tr.
Italian, 1 slice (4½″ × 3¼″ × ¾″)	0	.09	.06	.8	0
pumpernickel, 1 slice (5″ × 2″ × ¼″)	0	.07	.04	.4	0
raisin, 1 slice (18 slices per 1 lb. loaf)	tr.	.01	.02	.2	tr.
rye, light, 1 slice (4¾″ × 3¾″ × ⁷⁄₁₆″)	0	.05	.02	.4	0
Vienna, 1 slice (4¾″ × 4″ × ½″)	tr.	.07	.06	.6	tr.
white, firm-crumb, 1 slice (20 slices per 1 lb. loaf)	tr.	.06	.05	.6	tr.
white, firm-crumb, 1 slice (30 slices per 1 lb. loaf)	tr.	.04	.03	.4	tr.
white, soft-crumb, 1 slice (18 slices per 1 lb. loaf)	tr.	.06	.05	.6	tr.
white, soft-crumb, 1 slice (22 slices per 1 lb. loaf)	tr.	.05	.04	.5	tr.
whole wheat, firm-crumb, 1 slice (18 slices per lb.)	tr.	.06	.03	.7	tr.
whole wheat, soft-crumb, 1 slice (16 slices per lb.)	tr.	.09	.03	.8	tr.
Breadcrumbs, dry, grated, 1 cup	tr.	.22	.30	3.5	tr.
Breadcrumbs, from soft-crumb white bread, 1 cup	tr.	.11	.09	1.1	tr.

Bread sticks, regular, 10 sticks (4¼″ long × ½″)	tr.	.06	.07	1.0	tr.
Bread sticks, Vienna, 1 stick (6½″ long × 1¼″)	tr.	.02	.03	.3	tr.
Bread stuffing mix, coarse crumbs, dry, 1 cup	tr.	.15	.18	2.2	tr.
Bread stuffing mix, cubes, dry, 1 cup	tr.	.07	.08	1.0	tr.
Broadbeans, immature seeds, raw, 4 oz.	250	.32	.19	1.8	34
Broadbeans, mature seeds, dry, 4 oz.	80	.57	.34	2.8	n.a.
Broccoli, raw, 1 lb. (about 3 medium stalks)	11,340	.45	1.04	4.1	513
boiled, drained, 1 medium stalk	4,500	.16	.36	1.4	162
boiled, drained, cut stalks, 1 cup	3,880	.14	.31	1.2	140
frozen, boiled, drained, 1 stalk (4½″–5″ long)	570	.02	.03	.2	22
frozen, boiled, drained, chopped, 1 cup	4,810	.11	.22	.9	105
Brussels sprouts, raw, 1 lb. (about 24 sprouts)	2,490	.45	.73	4.1	463
boiled, drained, 4 sprouts (1¼″–1½″ diam.)	440	.07	.12	.7	73
boiled, drained, 1 cup	810	.12	.22	1.2	135
frozen, boiled, drained, 1 cup	880	.12	.16	.9	126
Buckwheat flour, dark, sifted, 1 cup	0	.57	.15	2.8	0
Buckwheat flour, light, sifted, 1 cup	0	.08	.04	.4	0
Bulgur, dry, club wheat, 1 cup	0	.53	.18	7.4	0
dry, hard red winter wheat, 1 cup	0	.48	.24	7.7	0
dry, white wheat, 1 cup	0	.47	.16	6.5	0
canned, seasoned, 1 cup	0	.08	.05	4.1	0
canned, unseasoned, 1 cup	0	.07	.04	3.2	0
Burbot, raw, meat only, 4 oz.	n.a.	.44	.16	1.7	n.a.
Butter, regular, 1 cup (2 sticks)	7,500	n.a.	n.a.	n.a.	0
regular, 1 tbsp.	470	n.a.	n.a.	n.a.	0
whipped, 1 cup	5,000	n.a.	n.a.	n.a.	0
whipped, 1 tbsp.	310	n.a.	n.a.	n.a.	0
Buttermilk, see Milk					

C

Cabbage, raw, fully trimmed, 1 lb.	590	.23	.23	1.4	213
raw, coarse, shredded or sliced, 1 cup	90	.04	.04	.2	33
raw, fine shredded or chopped, 1 cup	120	.05	.05	.3	42

FOOD AND MEASURE	Vit. A (I.U.)	Thia. (mg.)	Rib. (mg.)	Nia. (mg.)	Vit. C (mg.)
boiled until tender, drained, shredded, 1 cup	190	.06	.06	.4	48
boiled until tender, drained, wedges, 1 cup	200	.03	.03	.2	41
red, raw, fully trimmed, 1 lb.	180	.41	.27	1.8	277
red, raw, coarse shredded or sliced, 1 cup	30	.06	.04	.3	43
red, raw, fine shredded or chopped, 1 cup	40	.08	.05	.4	55
savoy, raw, fully trimmed, 1 lb.	910	.23	.36	1.4	249
savoy, raw, coarse shredded or sliced, 1 cup	140	.04	.06	.2	39
Cabbage, Chinese, raw, fully trimmed, 1 lb.	680	.23	.18	2.7	113
Cabbage, Chinese, raw, 1″ pieces, 1 cup	110	.04	.03	.5	19
Cabbage, spoon, raw, fully trimmed, 1 lb.	14,060	.23	.45	3.6	113
raw, 1″ pieces, 1 cup	2,170	.04	.07	.6	18
boiled, drained, 1″ pieces, 1 cup	5,270	.07	.14	1.2	26
Cakes, baked from mix as per directions:					
angel food, without icing, 3½-oz. serving	0	tr.	.11	.1	0
chocolate malt, white icing, 3½-oz. serving	190	.03	.07	.2	tr.
coffee cake, without icing, 3½-oz. serving	160	.18	.16	1.4	tr.
cup cake, without icing, 1 cup cake (2½″ diam.)	40	.01	.03	.1	tr.
cup cake, chocolate icing, 1 cup cake (2½″ diam.)	60	.01	.04	.1	tr.
devil's food, chocolate icing, 3½-oz. serving	150	.03	.08	.3	tr.
gingerbread, without icing, 3½-oz. serving	tr.	.03	.09	.8	tr.
honey-spice, caramel icing, 3½-oz. serving	160	.02	.09	.2	tr.
marble, white icing, 3½-oz. serving	90	.02	.08	.2	tr.
white, chocolate icing, 3½-oz. serving	60	.02	.08	.2	tr.

yellow, chocolate icing, 3½-oz. serving	140	.02	.08	.2	tr.
Candy:					
almonds, chocolate coated, 1 oz. (about 6–8 nuts)	tr.	.03	.15	.5	tr.
almonds, candy coated, 1 oz. (about 8 nuts)	0	.01	.08	.3	0
butterscotch, 1 oz.	40	0	tr.	tr.	0
chocolate, bittersweet, 1 oz.	10	.01	.05	.3	0
chocolate, milk, plain, 1 oz.	80	.02	.10	.1	tr.
chocolate, milk, candy-coated discs, 1 oz. (about 31)	30	.02	.06	.1	tr.
chocolate, milk, with almonds, 1 oz.	70	.02	.12	.2	tr.
chocolate, milk, with peanuts, 1 oz.	50	.07	.07	1.4	tr.
chocolate, semi-sweet, 1 oz.	10	tr.	.02	.1	tr.
chocolate, sweet, 1 oz.	tr.	.01	.04	.1	tr.
coconut, chocolate coated, 1 oz.	0	.01	.02	.1	0
fondant, chocolate coated, 1 oz.	tr.	.01	.02	tr.	tr.
fudge, chocolate, plain or with nuts, 1 oz.	tr.	.01	.03	.1	tr.
fudge, with caramel and peanuts, chocolate coated, 1 oz.	tr.	.07	.04	1.0	tr.
gum drops or jelly beans, 1 oz.	0	0	tr.	tr.	0
hard candy, 1 oz.	0	0	0	0	0
marshmallows, 1 oz.	0	0	tr.	tr.	0
mints, plain, 1 oz.	0	tr.	tr.	tr.	0
mints, chocolate coated, 1 oz.	tr.	.01	.02	tr.	tr.
peanut brittle, 1 oz.	0	.05	.01	1.0	0
peanuts, chocolate coated, 1 oz.	tr.	.01	.05	2.1	tr.
raisins, chocolate coated, 1 oz.	40	.02	.06	.1	tr.
vanilla creams, chocolate coated, 1 oz.	tr.	.01	.02	tr.	tr.
Cantaloupe, ½ melon (5″ diam.)	9,240	.11	.08	1.6	90
Cantaloupe, cubed, 1 cup	5,440	.06	.05	1.0	53
Carambola, fresh, 1 fruit (2½ oz.)	680	.02	.01	.2	20
Carissa, fresh, sliced, 1 cup	60	.06	.09	.3	57
Carrots, raw, 1 carrot (7½″ long)	7,930	.04	.04	.4	6
raw, grated or shredded, 1 cup	12,100	.07	.06	.7	9
boiled, drained, diced, 1 cup	15,230	.07	.07	.7	9
boiled, drained, sliced, 1 cup	16,280	.08	.08	.8	9
canned, 1 cup with liquid	24,600	.05	.05	1.0	5
canned, drained, diced, 1 cup	21,750	.03	.04	.6	3

FOOD AND MEASURE	Vit. A (I.U.)	Thia. (mg.)	Rib. (mg.)	Nia. (mg.)	Vit. C (mg.)
canned, drained, sliced, 1 cup	23,250	.03	.05	.6	3
dehydrated, 1 oz.	28,350	.09	.09	.9	4
Casaba melon, 1 wedge					
(7¾″ × 2″)	40	.06	.04	.8	18
Casaba melon, cubed, 1 cup	50	.07	.05	1.0	22
Cashew nuts, 1 lb.	450	1.95	1.13	8.2	n.a.
Cashew nuts, whole kernels, 1 cup	140	.60	.35	2.5	n.a.
Catsup, tomato, bottled, 1 cup	3,820	.25	.19	4.4	41
Catsup, tomato, bottled, 1 tbsp.	210	.01	.01	.2	2
Cauliflower, raw, 1 head					
(6″–7″ diam.)	520	.95	.86	6.0	671
raw, flowerbuds, sliced, 1 cup	50	.09	.09	.6	66
boiled, drained, 1 cup	80	.11	.10	.8	69
frozen, boiled, drained, 1 cup	50	.07	.09	.7	74
Celery, raw, 1 large outer stalk					
(8″ long)	110	.01	.01	.1	4
raw, 3 small inner stalks					
(5″ long)	140	.02	.02	.2	5
raw, chopped or diced, 1 cup	320	.04	.04	.4	11
cooked, diced, 1 cup	390	.03	.05	.5	9
Cereal, ready-to-eat (vitamin-enriched):					
bran flakes (40%), 1 cup	1,650	.41	.49	4.1	12
bran flakes with raisins, 1 cup	2,350	.58	.71	5.8	18
corn flakes, 1 cup	1,180	.29	.35	2.9	9
corn flakes, sugar coated, 1 cup	1,880	.46	.56	4.6	14
corn, puffed, 1 cup	940	.23	.28	2.3	7
corn, puffed, presweetened, 1 cup	1,410	.35	.42	3.5	11
corn, shredded, 1 cup	0	.11	.05	.5	0
oats, shredded, 1 cup	0	1.59	1.90	15.9	0
oats, puffed, 1 cup	1,180	.29	.35	2.9	9
oats with corn, puffed, 1 cup	1,650	.41	.49	4.1	12
rice, ovenpopped, 1 cup	1,410	.35	.42	3.5	11
rice, ovenpopped, presweetened,					
1 cup	2,120	.52	.63	5.2	16
rice, puffed, 1 cup	0	.07	.01	.7	0
rice, shredded, 1 cup	0	.10	.02	1.8	0
wheat flakes, 1 cup	1,410	.35	.42	3.5	11
wheat germ, toasted, 1 tbsp.	10	.11	.05	.3	1
wheat, puffed, 1 cup	0	.08	.03	1.2	0
Cereal, cooked (enriched):					
farina, regular, cooked, 1 cup	0	.10	.07	1.0	0

farina, quick, cooked, 1 cup	0	.12	.07	1.0	0
farina, instant, cooked, 1 cup	0	.17	.10	1.2	0
oat and wheat, cooked, 1 cup	0	.22	.07	1.2	0
oatmeal or rolled oats, cooked,					
1 cup	0	.19	.05	.2	0
rice, granulated, cooked, 1 cup	0	.15	.02	2.0	0
wheat, rolled, cooked, 1 cup	0	.17	.07	2.2	0
wheat, whole-meal, cooked, 1 cup	0	.15	.05	1.5	0
Chard, Swiss, raw, fully trimmed,					
1 lb.	28,480	.27	.77	2.3	145
boiled, drained, leaves and					
stalks, 1 cup	7,830	.06	.16	.6	23
boiled, drained, leaves, 1 cup	9,450	.07	.19	.7	28
Cheese, American, 1 oz.	350	.01	.12	tr.	0
American, shredded, 1 cup	1,380	.02	.46	tr.	0
blue or Roquefort, 1 oz.	350	.01	.17	.3	0
blue or Roquefort, crumbled,					
1 cup packed	3,090	.07	1.52	3.0	0
brick, 1 oz.	350	n.a.	.13	tr.	0
Camembert, domestic, 1 oz.	290	.01	.21	.2	0
Cheddar, domestic, 1 oz.	370	.01	.13	tr.	0
Cheddar, shredded, 1 cup	1,480	.03	.52	.1	0
cottage cheese, creamed, 1 oz.	50	.01	.07	tr.	0
cottage cheese, creamed, 1 cup					
packed	420	.07	.61	.2	0
cottage cheese, uncreamed, 1 oz.	tr.	.01	.08	tr.	0
cottage cheese, uncreamed,					
1 cup packed	20	.06	.56	.2	0
cream cheese, 1 oz.	440	.01	.07	tr.	0
cream cheese, regular, 1 tbsp.	220	tr.	.03	tr.	0
cream cheese, whipped, 1 tbsp.	150	tr.	.02	tr.	0
Limburger, 1 oz.	320	.02	.14	.1	0
Parmesan, 1 oz.	300	.01	.21	.1	0
Parmesan, shredded, 1 cup	910	.02	.62	.2	0
Parmesan, grated, 1 cup	1,260	.02	.87	.2	0
Parmesan, grated or shredded,					
1 tbsp.	60	tr.	.04	tr.	0
Swiss, domestic, 1 oz.	320	tr.	.11	tr.	0
Cheese food, American, 1 oz.	280	.01	.16	.1	0
Cheese food, American, 1 tbsp.	140	tr.	.08	tr.	0
Cheese spread, American, 5-oz.					
jar or can	1,240	.01	.77	.1	0
Cheese spread, American, 1 tbsp.	120	tr.	.08	tr.	0
Cheese straws, 10 pieces (5″ long)	230	.01	.10	.2	0

FOOD AND MEASURE	Vit. A (I.U.)	Thia. (mg.)	Rib. (mg.)	Nia. (mg.)	Vit. C (mg.)
Cherimoya, fresh, 1 fruit					
(5″ diam.)	50	.49	.54	6.3	44
Cherries, red sour, whole, 1 cup	1,030	.05	.06	.4	10
red sour, pitted, 1 cup	1,550	.08	.09	.6	16
sweet, whole, 1 cup	130	.06	.07	.5	12
sweet, pitted, 1 cup	160	.07	.09	.6	15
sweet, 10 cherries	70	.03	.04	.3	7
canned, red sour, water pack,					
1 cup with liquid	1,660	.07	.05	.5	12
canned, sweet, in syrup,					
1 cup with liquid	150	.05	.05	.5	8
canned, sweet, water pack,					
1 cup with liquid	150	.05	.05	.5	7
frozen, red sour, sweetened, 8 oz.	1,090	.07	.14	.7	14
frozen, red sour, unsweetened,					
8 oz.	2,270	.09	.16	.7	12
Chestnuts, fresh, in shell, 1 lb.	n.a.	.81	.81	2.2	n.a.
fresh, shelled, 1 lb.	n.a.	1.00	1.00	2.7	n.a.
fresh, shelled, 1 cup	n.a.	.35	.35	1.0	n.a.
Chicken, broiled, meat only, 4 oz.	102	.06	.22	10.0	n.a.
roasted, dark meat, 4 oz.	182	.14	.22	6.0	n.a.
roasted, dark meat, chopped					
or diced, 1 cup	220	.17	.27	7.4	n.a.
roasted, light meat, 4 oz.	125	.09	.11	13.4	n.a.
roasted, light meat, chopped or					
diced, 1 cup	150	.11	.14	16.5	n.a.
stewed, meat only, 4 oz.	282	.05	.17	10.9	n.a.
stewed, meat only, chopped or					
diced, 1 cup	350	.06	.22	13.4	n.a.
canned, meat only, 1 cup	470	.08	.25	9.0	8
Chicken gizzards, simmered,					
chopped or diced, 1 cup	n.a.	.03	.30	4.0	n.a.
Chicken liver, see Liver					
Chicken, potted, 1 cup	n.a.	.07	.50	2.7	n.a.
Chicken pot pie, frozen, 8 oz.	3,015	.25	.25	4.1	5
Chickpeas, dry, 1 cup	100	.62	.30	4.0	n.a.
Chili con carne, with beans,					
canned, 1 cup	150	.08	.18	3.3	n.a.
Chili powder, seasoned, dry, 1 tsp.	1,300	tr.	.02	.2	tr.
Chili sauce, hot, green pepper,					
canned, 1 cup	1,490	.07	.07	1.7	167

Chili sauce, hot, red pepper, canned, 1 cup	23,500	.02	.22	1.5	74
Chili sauce, tomato, bottled, 1 cup	3,820	.25	.19	4.4	44
Chili sauce, tomato, bottled, 1 tbsp.	210	.01	.01	.2	2
Chives, raw, 2 oz.	3,290	.05	.07	.3	32
Chives, raw, chopped, 1 tbsp.	170	tr.	tr.	tr.	2
Chocolate, baking or bitter, 1 oz.	20	.01	.07	.4	0
Chocolate, baking or bitter, grated, 1 cup	80	.07	.32	2.0	0
Chocolate, see Candy and Syrup					
Chow mein, chicken, canned, without noodles, 1 cup	150	.05	.10	1.0	13
Clams, raw, meat only, 1 pint (1 lb.)	450	.45	.82	5.9	45
Clams, canned, 8 oz. with liquid	n.a.	.02	.24	2.3	n.a.
Cocoa, dry powder, 1 tbsp.	tr.	.01	.02	.1	0
mix, 1 oz. (4 heaping tsp.)	n.a.	.01	.03	.1	0
mix, with nonfat dry milk, 1 oz. (4 heaping tsp.)	10	.04	.21	.2	1
Coconut, fresh, in shell, 1 coconut (1⅔ lb.)	0	.20	.08	2.0	12
fresh, meat only, 1 piece (2″ × 2″ × ½″)	0	.02	.01	.2	1
fresh, shredded or grated, 1 cup	0	.04	.02	.4	2
dried, unsweetened, 4 oz.	0	.07	.05	.7	0
Coconut cream (from grated coconut meat), 1 cup	0	.05	.02	1.2	2
Coconut water (liquid from coconut), 1 cup	0	tr.	tr.	.2	5
Cod, fresh, raw, meat only, 4 oz.	0	.07	.08	2.5	2
fresh, meat only, broiled with butter, 4 oz.	205	.09	.13	3.4	n.a.
dehydrated, lightly salted, shredded, 1 cup	0	.03	.19	4.6	n.a.
Coffee, instant, regular, dry, 1 tsp.	0	0	tr.	.2	0
Coffee, instant, freeze-dried, dry, 1 tsp.	0	0	tr.	.3	0
Coleslaw, commercial, made with mayonnaise, 1 cup	190	.06	.06	.4	35
Coleslaw, commercial, made with French dressing, 1 cup	130	.05	.05	.4	35
Collards, raw, leaves only, 1 lb.	42,180	.73	1.41	7.7	689
boiled in small amount water, drained, 1 cup	14,820	.21	.38	2.3	144
boiled in large amount water, drained, 1 cup	14,820	.13	.27	2.1	97

FOOD AND MEASURE	Vit. A (I.U.)	Thia. (mg.)	Rib. (mg.)	Nia. (mg.)	Vit. C (mg.)
frozen, chopped, boiled, drained, 1 cup	11,560	.10	.24	1.0	56
Cookies, commercial, animal crackers, 1 oz. (about 11 pcs.)	35	.01	.03	.1	tr.
brownies, frozen, 1 piece (1½″ × 1¾″ × ⅞″)	50	.02	.02	.1	tr.
butter thins, 1 oz. (about 6)	185	.01	.02	.1	0
chocolate chip, 10 pieces (2¼″ diam.)	130	.04	.07	.4	tr.
coconut bars, 10 pieces (3″ × 1¼″ × ¼″)	140	.04	.05	.4	0
fig bars, 4 pieces (1⅝″ square × ⅜″)	60	.02	.04	.2	tr.
gingersnaps, 10 pieces (2″ diam.)	50	.03	.04	.3	tr.
graham crackers, plain, 2 pieces (2½″ square)	0	.01	.03	.2	0
graham crackers, chocolate, 1 piece (2½″ × 2″ × ¼″)	10	.01	.04	.2	0
graham crackers, sugar-honey, 2 pieces (2½″ square)	n.a.	tr.	.02	.1	0
ladyfingers, 4 pieces (3¼″ × 1⅜″ × 1⅛″)	290	.03	.06	.1	0
macaroons, 2 pieces (2¾″ diam.)	0	.02	.06	.2	0
marshmallow, chocolate coated, 4 pieces (1¾″ diam.)	140	.01	.03	.1	tr.
marshmallow, coconut coated, 4 pieces (2⅛″ diam.)	190	.01	.04	.1	tr.
molasses, 1 piece (3⅝″ diam.)	30	.01	.02	.2	0
oatmeal with raisins, 4 pieces (2⅝″ diam.)	30	.06	.04	.3	tr.
peanut, sandwich type, 4 pieces (1¾″ diam.)	100	.03	.04	1.4	tr.
peanut, sugar wafer, 10 pieces (1¾″ × 1⅜″ × ⅜″)	140	.05	.06	2.0	tr.
raisin biscuit, 4 pieces (2¼″ × 2½″ × ¼″)	150	.03	.06	.4	tr.
sandwich, cream, 4 oval pieces (3⅛″ × 1¼″ × ⅜″)	0	.02	.02	.3	0
sandwich, cream, 4 round pieces (1¾″ diam.)	0	.02	.02	.2	0

shortbread, 10 pieces (1⅝″ square × ¼″)	60	.03	.04	.4	0
sugar, 10 pieces (2¼″ diam.)	90	.13	.13	1.0	tr.
sugar wafers, 10 pieces (3½″ × 1″ × ½″)	130	.01	.04	.5	0
vanilla wafers, 10 pieces (1¾″ diam.)	50	.01	.03	.1	0
vanilla, brown edge, 10 pieces (2¾″ diam.)	80	.01	.04	.2	0
Corn, on cob, boiled, drained, 1 ear (5″ long)	310	.09	.08	1.1	7
kernels, boiled, drained, 1 cup	660	.18	.17	2.1	12
canned, cream style, 1 cup	840	.08	.13	2.6	13
canned, kernel, vacuum pack, 1 cup	740	.06	.13	2.3	11
canned, kernel, wet pack, 1 cup with liquid	690	.08	.13	2.3	13
canned, kernel, wet pack, drained, 1 cup	580	.05	.08	1.5	7
frozen, on cob, boiled, drained, 1 ear (5″ long)	440	.18	.10	2.1	9
frozen, kernels, boiled, drained, 1 cup	580	.15	.10	2.5	8
Corn flour, 1 cup	400	.23	.07	1.6	0
Corn grits, degermed, enriched, dry, 1 cup	700	.70	.42	5.6	0
Corn grits, degermed, enriched, cooked, 1 cup	150	.10	.07	1.0	0
Cornmeal, whole ground, unbolted, dry, 1 cup	620	.46	.13	2.4	0
bolted, dry, 1 cup	590	.37	.10	2.3	0
degermed, dry, 1 cup	610	.61	.36	4.8	0
degermed, cooked, 1 cup	140	.14	.10	1.2	0
Cowpeas, immature seeds, raw, 1 cup	540	.62	.19	2.3	42
Cowpeas, immature seeds, boiled, drained, 1 cup	580	.50	.18	2.3	28
Cowpeas, immature seeds, canned, 1 cup with liquid	150	.23	.13	1.3	8
Cowpeas, immature seeds, frozen, boiled, drained, 1 cup	290	.68	.19	2.4	15
Cowpeas, young pods, boiled, drained, 8 oz.	3,175	.21	.21	1.8	39
Cowpeas, mature seeds, raw, 1 cup	50	1.79	.36	3.7	n.a.
Cowpeas, mature seeds, cooked, 1 cup	30	.40	.10	1.0	n.a.

113

FOOD AND MEASURE	Vit. A (I.U.)	Thia. (mg.)	Rib. (mg.)	Nia. (mg.)	Vit. C (mg.)
Crab, steamed, meat only, 4 oz.	2,460	.18	.09	3.1	2
steamed, meat only, flaked, 1 cup packed	4,560	.34	.17	5.9	4
canned, meat only, 1 cup packed	n.a.	.13	.13	3.0	n.a.
Crackers, commercial:					
animal, see Cookies					
butter, 10 rectangular pieces (2½″ × 1⅜″ × ⅛″)	80	tr.	.02	.4	0
butter, 10 round pieces (1⅞″ diam.)	70	tr.	.01	.3	0
cheese, 10 rectangular pieces (1⅝″ × ¼″)	30	tr.	.01	.1	0
cheese, 10 round pieces (1⅞″ diam.)	120	tr.	.03	.3	0
cheese, 10 square pieces (1″ square)	40	tr.	.01	.1	0
graham, see Cookies					
saltines or soda, 10 pieces (1⅞″ square)	0	tr.	.01	.3	0
sandwich, cheese-peanut butter, 4 pieces (1⅝″ square)	10	.01	.02	1.0	0
soup or oyster, 1 cup	0	tr.	.02	.5	0
Cranberries, raw, whole, 1 cup	40	.03	.02	.1	10
Cranberries, raw, chopped, 1 cup	45	.03	.02	.1	12
Cranberry juice cocktail, bottled, 1 cup	tr.	.03	.03	.1	40
Cranberry sauce, canned, sweetened, 1 cup	60	.03	.03	.1	6
Cranberry-orange relish, uncooked, 1 cup	190	.08	.06	.3	50
Crayfish, raw, meat only, 4 oz.	n.a.	.01	.05	2.2	n.a.
Cream, half and half, 1 cup	1,160	.07	.39	.1	2
half and half, 1 tbsp.	70	tr.	.02	tr.	tr.
light or coffee, 1 cup	2,020	.07	.36	.1	2
light or coffee, 1 tbsp.	130	tr.	.02	tr.	tr.
light whipping, 1 cup (2 cups whipped)	3,060	.05	.29	.1	2
light whipping, 1 tbsp. (2 tbsp. whipped)	190	tr.	.02	tr.	tr.
heavy whipping, 1 cup (2 cups whipped)	3,670	.05	.26	.1	2

114

heavy whipping, 1 tbsp. (2 tbsp. whipped)	230	tr.	.02	tr.	tr.
Cress, garden, raw, fully trimmed, 1 lb.	42,180	.36	1.18	4.5	313
boiled in small amount water, drained, 1 cup	10,400	.08	.22	1.1	46
boiled in large amount water, drained, 1 cup	9,450	.05	.20	.9	31
Cress, water, see Watercress					
Cucumbers, raw, with skin, 1 large (1½ per lb.)	750	.09	.12	.6	33
with skin, sliced (⅛" thick), 1 cup	260	.03	.04	.2	12
pared, 1 large (1½ per lb.)	tr.	.08	.11	.6	31
pared, sliced (⅛" thick), 1 cup	tr.	.04	.06	.3	15
Currants, black, fully trimmed, 4 oz. (about 1 cup)	260	.06	.06	.3	230
Currants, red or white, fully trimmed, 4 oz. (about 1 cup)	135	.05	.06	.1	47
Cusk, steamed, meat only, 4 oz.	n.a.	.04	.11	3.1	n.a.

D-E

Dandelion greens, raw, fully trimmed, 1 lb.	63,500	.86	1.18	n.a.	159
Dandelion greens, boiled, drained, 1 cup	12,290	.14	.17	n.a.	19
Danish pastry, plain, 1 piece (6½" × 2¾" × ¾")	230	.05	.11	.6	tr.
Danish pastry, plain, 1 piece (4½" diam.)	200	.04	.10	.5	tr.
Dates, domestic (moisturized), whole, 4 oz.	50	.09	.10	2.2	0
whole, 10 dates	40	.07	.08	1.8	0
pitted, 4 oz.	55	.10	.12	2.5	0
pitted, chopped, 1 cup	90	.16	.18	3.9	0
Dock or sorrel, raw, with stems, 1 lb.	40,960	.29	.70	1.6	378
Doughnuts, plain, cake type, 1 piece (3⅝" diam.; 2 oz.)	50	.09	.09	.7	tr.
cake type, 1 piece (1½" diam.; ½ oz.)	10	.02	.02	.2	tr.
yeast leavened, 1 piece (3¾" diam.; 1½ oz.)	30	.07	.07	.6	0
Drum, red, raw, meat only, 4 oz.	n.a.	.17	.06	4.0	n.a.
Duck, domestic, raw, meat only, 4 oz.	n.a.	.11	.14	8.8	n.a.

FOOD AND MEASURE	Vit. A (I.U.)	Thia. (mg.)	Rib. (mg.)	Nia. (mg.)	Vit. C (mg.)
Eclair, custard, iced, 1 piece (5″ × 2″ × 1¾″)	340	.04	.16	.1	tr.
Eel, domestic, raw, meat only, 4 oz.	1,835	.25	.41	1.6	n.a.
Eggs, chicken, raw, whole, 1 large	590	.05	.15	tr.	0
raw, whole, 1 medium	520	.05	.13	tr.	0
raw, white from 1 large egg	0	tr.	.09	tr.	0
raw, yolk from 1 large egg	580	.04	.07	tr.	0
boiled or poached, 1 large egg	590	.04	.14	tr.	0
fried in butter, 1 large egg	650	.05	.14	tr.	0
scrambled with milk, cooked in butter, 1 large egg	690	.05	.18	tr.	0
Eggplant, raw, whole, 1 lb.	30	.20	.17	2.3	19
Eggplant, boiled, drained, diced, 1 cup	20	.10	.08	1.0	6
Elderberries, fresh, whole, 1 lb.	2,560	.30	.27	2.3	154
Escarole, fresh, cut pieces, 1 cup	1,650	.04	.07	.3	5

F

FOOD AND MEASURE	Vit. A (I.U.)	Thia. (mg.)	Rib. (mg.)	Nia. (mg.)	Vit. C (mg.)
Farina, see Cereal, cooked					
Fat, cooking, 1 cup	n.a.	0	0	0	0
Fennel leaves, raw, fully trimmed, 4 oz.	3,990	n.a.	n.a.	n.a.	35
Figs, raw, whole, 1 large (2½″ diam.; 7 per lb.)	50	.04	.03	.3	1
Figs, canned, in syrup, 1 cup with liquid	80	.08	.08	.5	3
Figs, canned, water pack, 1 cup with liquid	70	.07	.07	.5	2
Filberts (hazelnuts), in shell, 1 lb.	n.a.	.96	n.a.	1.9	tr.
shelled, 1 lb.	n.a.	2.09	n.a.	4.1	tr.
shelled, chopped, 1 cup	n.a.	.53	n.a.	1.0	tr.
Finnan haddie (smoked haddock), meat only, 4 oz.	n.a.	.07	.06	2.4	n.a.
Fish, see individual listings					
Fish sticks, breaded, frozen, 1-oz. stick	0	.01	.02	.5	n.a.
Flounder, raw, meat only, 4 oz.	0	.06	.06	1.9	n.a.
Flounder, baked with butter, meat only, 4 oz.	n.a.	.08	.09	2.8	2
Flour, see individual listings					
Frankfurters, packaged, 1-lb. package	n.a.	.73	.91	12.2	n.a.

Frankfurters, packaged,					
1 frankfurter (2 oz.)	n.a.	.09	.11	1.5	n.a.
Frog legs, raw, meat only, 4 oz.	0	.16	.28	1.4	n.a.
Fruit, see individual listings					
Fruit cocktail, canned in syrup,					
1 cup with liquid	360	.05	.03	1.0	5
Fruit cocktail, canned, water pack,					
1 cup with liquid	370	.05	.02	1.2	5
Fruit salad, canned in syrup,					
1 cup with liquid	1,150	.03	.08	1.5	5
Fruit salad, canned, water pack,					
1 cup with liquid	1,150	.02	.07	1.5	7

G

Garlic, raw, 1 oz.	tr.	.07	.02	.1	4
Garlic, raw, 1 clove (1¼″ × ⅝″					
× ⅜″)	tr.	.01	tr.	tr.	tr.
Gingerroot, fresh, scraped, 4 oz.	11	.02	.05	.8	5
Goose, domestic, raw, meat only,					
4 oz.	n.a.	.12	.18	10.6	n.a.
Gooseberries, fresh, trimmed, 1 cup	440	n.a.	n.a.	n.a.	50
Grandilla, purple, 1 fruit (1¼ oz.)	130	tr.	.02	.3	5
Grapefruit, pink, seeded, ½ large					
(4⅜″ diam.)	750	.07	.03	.3	67
pink, seedless, ½ large					
(4″ diam.)	600	.05	.03	.3	49
pink, sections, 1 cup	880	.08	.04	.4	78
white, seeded, ½ large					
(4⅜″ diam.)	20	.06	.03	.3	61
white, seedless, ½ large					
(4″ diam.)	10	.05	.03	.3	49
white, sections, 1 cup	20	.08	.04	.4	74
canned, in syrup, 1 cup					
with liquid	30	.08	.05	.5	76
canned, water pack, 1 cup					
with liquid	20	.07	.05	.5	73
Grapefruit juice, fresh, 1 cup	200	.10	.05	.5	93
canned, sweetened, 1 cup	30	.08	.05	.5	78
canned, unsweetened, 1 cup	20	.07	.05	.5	84
frozen, sweetened, diluted,					
1 cup	20	.08	.03	.4	82
frozen, unsweetened, diluted,					
1 cup	20	.10	.04	.5	96
Grapefruit-orange juice, canned,					
1 cup	250	.12	.05	.5	84

FOOD AND MEASURE	Vit. A (I.U.)	Thia. (mg.)	Rib. (mg.)	Nia. (mg.)	Vit. C (mg.)
Grape, Concord, Delaware, etc.,					
whole, 1 cup	100	.05	.03	.3	4
Thompson seedless, etc.,					
whole, 1 cup	160	.08	.05	.5	6
Tokay, Emperor, etc., seeded,					
whole, 1 cup	150	.08	.05	.5	6
halves, 1 cup	180	.09	.05	.5	7
canned, Thompson seedless,					
in syrup, 1 cup	180	.10	.03	.5	5
canned, Thompson seedless,					
water pack, 1 cup	170	.10	.02	.5	5
Grape juice, canned, 1 cup	n.a.	.10	.05	.5	tr.
Grape juice, frozen, sweetened,					
diluted, 1 cup	10	.05	.08	.5	10
Grape drink, canned, 1 cup	n.a.	.03	.03	.3	40
Groundcherries, fresh, trimmed,					
1 cup	1,010	.15	.06	3.9	15
Guava, raw, 4 oz.	320	.06	.06	1.4	275
Guava, strawberry, raw, whole,					
4 oz.	102	.03	.03	.7	42

H

FOOD AND MEASURE	Vit. A (I.U.)	Thia. (mg.)	Rib. (mg.)	Nia. (mg.)	Vit. C (mg.)
Haddock, raw, meat only, 4 oz.	n.a.	.05	.08	3.4	n.a.
Haddock, breaded, fried, 4 oz.	n.a.	.05	.08	3.6	2
Halibut, raw, meat only, 4 oz.	500	.08	.08	9.5	n.a.
Halibut, broiled with butter, 4 oz.	770	.06	.08	9.4	n.a.
Ham, meat only, boiled, 4 oz.	0	.50	.17	3.0	n.a.
fresh, medium-fat, roasted, 4 oz.	0	.73	.33	6.5	n.a.
light cure, medium-fat, roasted,					
4 oz.	0	.54	.21	4.1	n.a.
light cure, lean, roasted, 4 oz.	0	.66	.26	5.1	n.a.
picnic, medium-fat, roasted,					
4 oz.	0	.59	.23	4.6	n.a.
picnic, lean, roasted, 4 oz.	0	.74	.30	5.7	n.a.
Ham, deviled, canned, 1 cup	0	.32	.23	3.6	n.a.
Ham, deviled, canned, 1 tbsp.	0	.02	.01	.2	n.a.
Ham, spiced, canned, 2 oz.	0	.18	.12	1.8	n.a.
Headcheese, 4 oz.	0	.05	.11	1.0	n.a.
Heart, beef, lean, braised, 4 oz.	35	.29	1.39	8.7	1
calf, braised, 4 oz.	45	.33	1.64	9.2	tr.
chicken, braised, 4 oz.	35	.07	1.01	6.1	5

lamb, braised, 4 oz.	114	.24	1.17	7.3	tr.
turkey, braised, 4 oz.	35	.29	1.12	6.5	5
Herring, Atlantic, raw, meat only,					
4 oz.	125	.02	.17	4.1	n.a.
Pacific, raw, meat only, 4 oz.	114	.02	.18	4.0	3
canned in tomato sauce, 4 oz.	n.a.	n.a.	.13	4.0	n.a.
canned, smoked (kippered),					
drained, 4 oz.	35	n.a.	.32	3.8	n.a.
Honey, strained or extracted, 1 cup	0	.02	.14	1.0	3
Honey, strained or extracted, 1 tbsp.	0	tr.	.01	.1	tr.
Honeydew melon, 1 wedge					
(7″ long × 2″ wide)	60	.06	.04	.9	34
Honeydew melon, cubes, 1 cup	70	.07	.05	1.0	39
Horseradish, raw, peeled, 2 oz.	n.a.	.12	n.a.	n.a.	134

I-J

Ice cream, regular (about 10%					
fat), 1 cup	590	.05	.28	.1	1
regular (about 12% fat), 1 cup	728	.05	.26	.1	1
regular, rich (about 16% fat),					
1 cup	980	.03	.16	.1	1
soft-serve (frozen custard),					
1 cup	760	.07	.36	.2	2
Ice cream cone, 2 oz.	1	.03	.12	.3	tr.
Ice milk, hardened (5.1% fat),					
1 cup	280	.07	.29	.1	1
Ice milk, soft-serve, 1 cup	370	.09	.39	.2	2
Ices, water, lime, 1 cup	tr.	tr.	tr.	tr.	2
Icing, mix, prepared, chocolate fudge,					
1 cup	840	.03	.12	.6	0
creamy fudge, made with water,					
1 cup	tr.	.05	.20	.7	tr.
creamy fudge, made with water					
and butter, 1 cup	960	.05	.17	.7	tr.
Jams and preserves, all flavors,					
1 tbsp.	tr.	tr.	.01	tr.	tr.
Jellies, all flavors, 1 tbsp.	tr.	tr.	.01	tr.	1

K-L

Kale, raw, leaves without stems,					
1 lb.	45,360	.73	1.18	9.5	844
leaves, boiled, drained, 1 cup	9,130	.11	.20	1.8	102
leaves, frozen, boiled, drained,					
1 cup	10,660	.08	.20	.9	49

119

FOOD AND MEASURE	Vit. A (I.U.)	Thia. (mg.)	Rib. (mg.)	Nia. (mg.)	Vit. C (mg.)
Kidney, beef, braised, 4 oz.	1,311	.58	5.49	12.2	n.a.
Kidney, beef, braised, ½″ pieces,					
1 cup	1,610	.71	6.75	15.0	n.a.
Knockwurst, 4 oz.	n.a.	.19	.24	2.9	n.a.
Kohlrabi, raw, diced, 1 cup	30	.08	.06	.4	92
Kohlrabi, boiled, drained, diced,					
1 cup	30	.10	.05	.3	71
Kumquats, fresh, 1 fruit (¾ oz.)	110	.01	.02	n.a.	7
Lamb, chop, loin, broiled, lean and					
fat, 4.8 oz.	n.a.	.16	.31	6.8	n.a.
chop, loin, broiled, lean only,					
4.8 oz.	n.a.	.20	.38	8.3	n.a.
chop, rib, boned, broiled, lean and					
fat, 4 oz.	0	.08	.13	3.0	0
chop, rib, boned, broiled, lean					
only, 4 oz.	n.a.	.19	.27	6.3	n.a.
leg, roasted, lean and fat, 4 oz.	n.a.	.17	.31	6.2	n.a.
leg, roasted, lean only, 4 oz.	n.a.	.18	.34	7.0	n.a.
shoulder, roasted, lean and fat,					
4 oz.	n.a.	.15	.26	5.3	n.a.
shoulder, roasted, lean only,					
4 oz.	n.a.	.17	.32	6.5	n.a.
Lambsquarter, raw, trimmed, 1 lb.	52,620	.70	2.00	5.5	363
Lambsquarter, boiled, drained,					
4 oz.	11,058	.11	.30	1.0	42
Lard, 1 cup	0	0	0	0	0
Leeks, raw, bulb and lower leaf					
portion, 4 oz.	23	.07	.03	.3	10
Lemon, fresh, whole, 1 lemon					
(2¼″ diam.)	40	.06	.05	.3	99
Lemon juice, fresh or canned, 1 cup	50	.07	.02	.2	112
fresh or canned, 1 tbsp.	tr.	tr.	tr.	tr.	7
frozen, single-strength, 6-oz. can	40	.05	.02	.2	81
Lemon peel, fresh, grated, 1 tbsp.	tr.	tr.	tr.	tr.	8
Lemonade, frozen, diluted, 1 cup	10	.01	.02	.2	17
Lentils, whole, dry, 1 cup	110	.70	.42	3.8	n.a.
Lentils, whole, cooked, 1 cup	40	.14	.12	1.2	0
Lettuce, Boston or bibb, 1 head					
(5″ diam.)	1,580	.10	.10	.5	13
Boston or bibb, 1 large or					
2 medium leaves	150	.01	.01	tr.	1

Boston or bibb, shredded pieces, 1 cup	530	.03	.03	.2	4
iceberg, 1 head (6″ diam.)	1,780	.32	.32	1.6	32
iceberg, 1 leaf (5″ × 4½″)	70	.01	.01	.1	1
iceberg, small chunks, 1 cup	250	.05	.05	.2	5
iceberg, shredded pieces, 1 cup	180	.03	.03	.2	3
romaine or looseleaf, shredded pieces, 1 cup	1,050	.03	.04	.2	10
Lime, fresh, pulp only, 1 lime (2″ diam.)	10	.02	.01	.1	25
Lime juice, fresh, 1 cup	20	.05	.02	.2	79
fresh, 1 tbsp.	tr.	tr.	tr.	tr.	5
canned, 1 cup	20	.05	.02	.2	52
Limeade, frozen, diluted, 1 cup	tr.	tr.	tr.	tr.	6
Liver, beef, fried, 4 oz.	60,555	.29	4.75	18.7	31
calf, fried, 4 oz.	37,083	.27	2.73	18.7	42
chicken, simmered, 4 oz.	13,948	.19	3.05	13.3	18
chicken, simmered, chopped, 1 cup	17,220	.24	3.77	16.4	22
hog, fried, 4 oz.	16,898	.39	4.95	25.3	25
lamb, broiled, 4 oz.	84,483	.56	5.79	28.2	41
turkey, simmered, 4 oz.	19,845	.18	2.37	16.2	n.a.
turkey, simmered, chopped, 1 cup	24,500	.22	2.93	20.0	n.a.
Liver paste, see Pâté de foie gras					
Liverwurst, fresh, 4 oz.	7,239	.23	1.48	6.5	n.a.
Liverwurst, smoked, 4 oz.	7,444	.19	1.64	9.4	n.a.
Lobster, northern, cooked, meat only, 4 oz.	n.a.	.11	.08	n.a.	n.a.
Lobster, cooked or canned, meat only, 1 cup	n.a.	.15	.10	n.a.	n.a.
Loganberries, fresh, trimmed, 1 cup	290	.04	.06	.6	35
Loganberries, canned, in syrup, 4 oz. with liquid	150	.01	.02	.2	9
Loquats, fresh, trimmed, 1 lb.	830	n.a.	n.a.	n.a.	1
Lychees, raw, 10 fruits (about 5¼ oz.)	n.a.	n.a.	.05	n.a.	38

M

Macadamia nuts, 6 nuts	0	.04	.01	.8	0
Macaroni, cooked 8–10 minutes, drained, 1 cup	0	.23	.13	1.8	0
Macaroni, cooked 14–20 minutes, drained, 1 cup	0	.20	.11	1.5	0

FOOD AND MEASURE	Vit. A (I.U.)	Thia. (mg.)	Rib. (mg.)	Nia. (mg.)	Vit. C (mg.)
Macaroni and cheese, canned, 1 cup	260	.12	.24	1.0	tr.
Mackerel, Atlantic, broiled with butter, 4 oz.	600	.17	.30	8.6	n.a.
Atlantic, canned, 4 oz. with liquid	490	.07	.24	6.6	n.a.
Pacific, canned, 4 oz. with liquid	34	.03	.38	10.0	n.a.
Mamey apple, fresh, whole, 1 fruit (3.1 lbs.)	2,010	.17	.35	3.5	122
Mango, fresh, whole, 1 fruit (10.2 oz.)	11,090	.12	.12	2.5	81
Mango, fresh, diced or sliced, 1 cup	7,920	.08	.08	1.8	58
Margarine, regular, 1 cup (2 sticks)	7,500	n.a.	n.a.	n.a.	0
regular, 1 tbsp.	470	n.a.	n.a.	n.a.	0
whipped, 1 cup	5,000	n.a.	n.a.	n.a.	0
whipped, 1 tbsp.	310	n.a.	n.a.	n.a.	0
Marmalade, citrus, 1 tbsp.	n.a.	tr.	tr.	tr.	1
Mayonnaise, see Salad dressings					
Meat, see individual listings					
Meat loaf, luncheon meat, 4 oz.	n.a.	.15	.25	2.8	n.a.
Meat, potted, 1 cup	n.a.	.07	.50	2.7	n.a.
Meat, potted, 1 tbsp.	n.a.	tr.	.03	.2	n.a.
Milk, cow's, whole (3.5% fat), 1 cup	350	.07	.41	.2	2
buttermilk, 1 cup	10	.10	.44	.2	2
skim, 1 cup	10	.09	.44	.2	2
skim, low-fat (2% nonfat milk solids added), 1 cup	200	.10	.52	.2	2
canned, condensed, sweetened, 1 cup	1,100	.24	1.16	.6	3
canned, evaporated, unsweetened, 1 cup	810	.10	.86	.5	3
dry, whole, regular, 1 cup powder	1,450	.37	1.87	.9	8
dry, nonfat, regular, 1 cup powder	40	.42	2.16	1.1	8
dry, nonfat, instant, 1 envelope (3.2 oz.)	30	.32	1.62	.8	6
Milk, goat's, 1 cup	390	.10	.27	.7	2
Milk, chocolate, commercial, with skim milk, 1 cup	210	.10	.40	.3	3

Milk, chocolate, commercial, with whole milk, 1 cup	330	.08	.40	.3	3
Milk, malted, dry, 1 oz. powder (about 3 heaping tsp.)	290	.09	.15	.1	0
Milk, malted, prepared with milk, 1 cup	590	.14	.49	.2	2
Muffin, corn, mix, baked 1 muffin (from ¼ cup batter)	100	.07	.08	.6	tr.
Mushrooms, raw, trimmed, 1 lb.	tr.	.45	2.09	19.1	14
Mushrooms, raw, sliced or diced, 1 cup	tr.	.07	.32	2.9	2
Mussels, raw, meat only, 4 oz.	n.a.	.18	.24	n.a.	n.a.
Mustard greens, raw, trimmed, 1 lb.	31,750	.50	1.00	3.6	440
Mustard greens, leaves, boiled, drained, 1 cup	8,120	.11	.20	.8	67
Mustard greens, frozen, chopped, boiled, drained, 1 cup	9,000	.05	.15	.6	30
Mustard spinach, raw, trimmed, 1 lb.	44,910	n.a.	n.a.	n.a.	590
Mustard spinach, boiled, drained, 1 cup	14,760	n.a.	n.a.	n.a.	117

N-O

Nectarine, fresh, 1 fruit (2½" diam.; 3 per lb.)	2,280	n.a.	n.a.	n.a.	18
New Zealand spinach, raw, trimmed, 1 lb.	19,500	.18	.77	2.7	136
New Zealand spinach, boiled, drained, 1 cup	6,480	.05	.18	.9	25
Noodles, egg, cooked, 1 cup	110	.22	.13	1.9	0
Ocean perch, Atlantic, raw, meat only, 4 oz.	n.a.	.11	.09	2.2	n.a.
Oil, cooking or salad, 1 cup	n.a.	0	0	0	0
Okra, raw, crosscut slices, 1 cup	520	.17	.21	1.0	31
boiled, drained, 10 pods (3" long × ⅝")	520	.14	.19	1.0	21
boiled, drained, crosscut slices, 1 cup	780	.21	.29	1.4	32
frozen, cuts, boiled, drained, 1 cup	890	.26	.31	1.9	22
Olives, canned or bottled, green, 10 large	120	n.a.	n.a.	n.a.	n.a.
ripe, Ascolano or Mission, 10 extra large	30	tr.	tr.	n.a.	n.a.

FOOD AND MEASURE	Vit. A (I.U.)	Thia. (mg.)	Rib. (mg.)	Nia. (mg.)	Vit. C (mg.)
ripe, Manzanillo, 10 large	20	tr.	tr.	n.a.	n.a.
ripe, Sevillano, 10 giant	40	tr.	tr.	n.a.	n.a.
Onion, mature, raw, 1 onion					
(2½" diam.)	40	.04	.04	.2	11
raw, chopped, 1 cup	70	.05	.07	.3	17
raw, sliced, 1 cup	50	.03	.05	.2	12
raw, chopped or minced, 1 tbsp.	tr.	tr.	tr.	tr.	1
boiled, drained, sliced or whole,					
1 cup	80	.06	.06	.4	15
Onion, young green, whole, 1 lb.	9,070	.23	.23	1.8	145
whole, chopped or sliced, 1 cup	2,000	.05	.05	.4	32
bulb and white top, 2 medium or					
6 small	tr.	.02	.01	.1	8
bulb and white top, chopped or					
sliced, 1 cup	tr.	.05	.04	.4	25
top only (green), chopped, 1 cup	4,000	.07	.10	.6	51
top only (green), chopped, 1 tbsp.	240	tr.	.01	tr.	3
Oranges, fresh, California navel,					
1 orange (2⅞" diam.)	280	.14	.06	.6	85
California navel, sections, 1 cup	330	.17	.07	.7	101
California Valencia, 1 orange					
(2⅝" diam.)	240	.12	.05	.5	59
California Valencia, sections,					
1 cup	360	.18	.07	.7	88
Florida, 1 orange (2⅝" diam.)	300	.15	.06	.6	68
Florida, sections, 1 cup	370	.19	.07	.7	83
Orange juice, fresh, 1 cup	500	.22	.07	1.0	124
canned, unsweetened, 1 cup	500	.17	.05	.7	100
frozen, unsweetened, diluted,					
1 cup	540	.23	.03	.9	120
Orange peel, fresh, 1 oz.	120	.03	.03	.3	39
Orange peel, fresh, grated, 1 tbsp.	30	.01	.01	.1	8
Orange-apricot juice drink,					
canned, 1 cup	1,440	.05	.02	.5	n.a.
Orange-grapefruit juice, see					
Grapefruit-orange juice					
Oysters, Eastern, raw, meat only,					
4 oz.	352	.16	.21	2.8	n.a.
meat only, 1 cup (13–19 medium					
oysters)	740	.34	.43	6.0	n.a.
frozen, 8 oz. with liquid	705	.32	.41	5.7	n.a.

Pancakes, baked from mix (enriched), 4″ diam. cake:				
plain and buttermilk	70	.04	.06	.2	tr.
buckwheat and other flours	60	.03	.04	.2	tr.
Papaya, fresh, whole 1 lb. papaya (3½″ diam.)	5,320	.12	.12	.9	170
fresh, cubed, 1 cup	2,450	.06	.06	.4	78
fresh, mashed, 1 cup	4,030	.09	.09	.7	129
Parsley, fresh, trimmed, 1 lb.	38,560	.54	1.18	5.4	780
fresh, 10 sprigs (2½″ long)	850	.01	.03	.1	17
fresh, chopped, 1 tbsp.	300	tr.	.01	tr.	6
Parsnips, boiled, drained, 1 small (6″ long)	10	.02	.03	tr.	4
boiled, drained, diced, 1 cup	50	.11	.12	.2	16
boiled, drained, mashed, 1 cup	60	.15	.17	.2	21
Pastina, egg, enriched, dry, 1 cup	370	1.50	.65	10.2	0
Pâté de foie gras, canned, 1 tbsp.	n.a.	.01	.04	.3	n.a.
Peach, fresh, whole, 1 peach (2½″ diam.)	1,330	.02	.05	1.0	7
fresh, pared, sliced, 1 cup	2,260	.03	.09	1.7	12
canned in syrup, 1 cup with liquid	1,100	.03	.05	1.5	8
canned, water pack, 1 cup with liquid	1,100	.02	.07	1.5	7
dehydrated nuggets, uncooked, 1 cup	5,000	tr.	.10	7.8	14
dehydrated nuggets, cooked, sweetened, 1 cup	2,580	tr.	.06	4.9	6
dried halves, 10 large halves	5,660	.01	.28	7.7	26
dried halves, 1 cup	6,240	.02	.30	8.5	29
dried halves, cooked, sweetened, 1 cup	2,890	.01	.14	3.8	5
dried halves, cooked, unsweetened, 1 cup	3,050	.01	.15	3.8	5
frozen, sliced, sweetened, 1 cup	1,630	.03	.10	1.8	100
Peach nectar, canned, 1 cup	1,070	.02	.05	1.0	tr.
Peanut butter, commercial, 1 tbsp.	n.a.	.02	.02	2.4	0
Peanuts, roasted, in shell, 1 lb.	n.a.	.97	.40	52.0	0
roasted, 10 nuts	n.a.	.06	.02	3.1	0
roasted, shelled, 1 cup	n.a.	.46	.19	24.8	0
roasted, shelled, chopped, 1 tbsp.	n.a.	.03	.01	1.5	0
Pear, fresh, Bartletts, whole, 1 pear (2½″ diam.)	30	.03	.07	.2	7

FOOD AND MEASURE	Vit. A (I.U.)	Thia. (mg.)	Rib. (mg.)	Nia. (mg.)	Vit. C (mg.)
fresh, Boscs, whole, 1 pear (2½″ diam.)	30	.03	.06	.1	6
fresh, D'Anjous, whole, 1 pear (3″ diam.)	40	.04	.08	.2	8
fresh, sliced or cubed, 1 cup	30	.03	.07	.2	7
canned in syrup, halves, 1 cup with liquid	10	.03	.05	.3	3
canned, water pack, halves, 1 cup with liquid	10	.02	.05	.2	2
dried halves, 10 halves	120	.02	.32	1.1	12
dried halves, 1 cup	130	.02	.32	1.1	13
dried halves, cooked, sweetened, 1 cup	80	.01	.20	.6	6
dried halves, cooked, unsweetened, 1 cup	80	.01	.20	.8	5
Pear nectar, canned, 1 cup	tr.	tr.	.05	tr.	tr.
Peas, blackeye, see Cowpeas					
Peas, green, immature, shelled, raw, 1 cup	930	.51	.20	4.2	39
boiled, drained, 1 cup	860	.45	.18	3.7	32
canned, Alaska or early, 1 cup with liquid	1,120	.22	.12	2.2	22
canned, Alaska or early, drained, 1 cup	1,170	.15	.10	1.4	14
canned, sweet, 1 cup with liquid	1,120	.27	.15	2.5	22
canned, sweet, drained, 1 cup	1,170	.19	.10	1.7	14
frozen, boiled, drained, 1 cup	960	.43	.14	2.7	21
Peas, mature seeds, whole or split, dry, 1 cup	240	1.48	.58	6.0	n.a.
Peas, mature seeds, split, cooked, 1 cup	80	.30	.18	1.8	n.a.
Peas and carrots, frozen, boiled, drained, 1 cup	14,880	.30	.11	2.1	13
Pecans, in shell, 1 lb.	310	2.07	.31	2.2	5
shelled, 1 lb.	590	3.90	.59	4.1	9
shelled, halves, 1 cup	140	.93	.14	1.0	2
shelled, chopped or pieces, 1 cup	150	1.01	.15	1.1	2
Pepper, hot chili, green, raw, seeded, 4 oz.	878	.10	.07	1.9	268
green, pods, canned, 4 oz. with liquid	695	.02	.06	.9	78

red, raw, pods with seeds, 4 oz.	24,624	.25	.41	5.0	421
red, raw, pods, seeded, 4 oz.	24,624	.11	.23	3.3	421
Pepper, sweet, green, raw, whole,					
1 pepper (2½″ diam.)	310	.06	.06	.4	94
green, raw, strips, 1 cup	420	.08	.08	.5	128
green, raw, sliced, 1 cup	340	.06	.06	.4	102
green, raw, chopped or diced,					
1 cup	630	.12	.12	.8	192
green, boiled, drained, 1 pepper					
(2½″ diam.)	310	.05	.05	.4	70
red, raw, whole, 1 pepper					
(2½″ diam.)	3,280	.06	.06	.4	151
red, raw, strips, 1 cup	4,450	.08	.08	.5	204
red, raw, sliced, 1 cup	3,560	.06	.06	.4	163
red, raw, chopped or diced, 1 cup	6,680	.12	.12	.8	306
Perch, yellow, raw, meat only, 4 oz.	n.a.	.07	.19	2.0	n.a.
Persimmon, Japanese (kaki),					
1 fruit (2½″ diam.)	4,550	.05	.03	.2	18
Pickle, cucumber, dill, 1 large					
(4″ long)	140	tr.	.03	tr.	8
dill, crosscut slices, 1 cup	160	tr.	.03	tr.	9
fresh, bread and butter, sliced,					
1 cup	240	tr.	.05	tr.	15
sour, 1 large (4″ long)	140	tr.	.03	tr.	9
sweet, gherkin, 1 small					
(2½″ long)	10	tr.	tr.	tr.	1
sweet, chopped, 1 cup	140	tr.	.03	tr.	10
Pie, apple, frozen, baked, 1 pie					
(8″ diam.)	70	.09	.08	.9	6
cherry, frozen, baked, 1 pie					
(8″ diam.)	1,850	.12	.11	1.4	14
coconut custard, frozen, baked,					
1 pie (8″ diam.)	960	.24	.96	1.2	tr.
coconut custard, mix, baked,					
1 pie (8″ diam.)	1,670	.24	1.12	1.6	tr.
Pie crust, mix, baked, 11.3 oz.					
(from 10-oz. package)	0	.10	.10	1.6	0
Pimientos, canned, 4-oz. can or jar	2,600	.02	.07	.5	107
Pimientos, canned, drained,					
1 average pimiento	920	.01	.02	.2	38
Pineapple, fresh, sliced, 1 slice					
(3½″ diam.)	60	.08	.03	.2	14
fresh, diced, 1 cup	110	.14	.05	.3	26
canned in syrup, chunk or					
crushed, 1 cup	130	.20	.05	.5	18

FOOD AND MEASURE	Vit. A (I.U.)	Thia. (mg.)	Rib. (mg.)	Nia. (mg.)	Vit. C (mg.)
canned in syrup, 1 large slice; 2¼ tbsp. liquid	50	.08	.02	.2	7
canned, water pack, tidbits, 1 cup	120	.20	.05	.5	17
frozen, chunks, sweetened, 1 cup	70	.25	.07	.7	20
Pineapple juice, canned, unsweetened, 1 cup	130	.13	.05	.5	23
Pineapple juice, frozen, unsweetened, diluted, 1 cup	30	.18	.05	.5	30
Pineapple-grapefruit juice drink, canned, 1 cup	30	.05	.03	.3	n.a.
Pineapple-orange juice drink, canned, 1 cup	130	.05	.03	.3	n.a.
Pine nuts, pignolias, shelled, 1 lb.	n.a.	2.88	n.a.	n.a.	n.a.
piñon, in shell, 1 lb.	80	3.37	.61	11.8	tr.
piñon, shelled, 1 lb.	160	5.75	1.12	20.8	tr.
Pistachio nuts, in shell, 1 lb.	520	1.52	n.a.	3.2	0
Pistachio nuts, shelled, 1 lb.	1,040	3.04	n.a.	6.4	0
Pitanga, pitted, 1 cup	2,550	.05	.07	.5	51
Pizza, cheese, chilled, baked, 1 pizza (12″ diam.)	1,880	.29	.77	4.8	29
Pizza, cheese, frozen, baked, 1 pizza (10″ diam.)	1,750	.24	.68	3.8	21
Plums, fresh, Damson, 10 plums (1″ diam.)	300	.08	.03	.5	n.a.
fresh, Damson, pitted, halves, 1 cup	510	.14	.05	.9	n.a.
fresh, Japanese, hybrid, 1 plum (2⅛″ diam.)	160	.02	.02	.3	4
fresh, Japanese, hybrid, pitted, halves, 1 cup	460	.06	.06	.9	11
fresh, prune type, 1 plum (1½″ diam.)	80	.01	.01	.1	1
fresh, prune type, pitted, halves, 1 cup	500	.05	.05	.8	7
canned in syrup, purple, whole, 1 cup	3,130	.05	.05	1.0	5
canned, water pack, purple, whole, 1 cup	3,110	.05	.05	1.0	5
Pokeberry shoots, boiled, drained, 1 cup	14,360	.12	.41	1.8	135
Pomegranate, fresh, whole, 1 fruit (3⅜″ diam.)	tr.	.05	.05	.5	6

Pompano, fresh, raw, meat only, 4 oz.	n.a.	.47	.25	n.a.	n.a.
Popcorn, popped, oil and salt added, 1 cup	n.a.	n.a.	.01	.2	0
Popcorn, popped, sugar-coated, 1 cup	n.a.	n.a.	.02	.4	0
Pork, chop, loin, broiled, lean and fat, 2.7 oz. chop	0	.75	.22	4.5	n.a.
chop, loin, broiled, lean only, 2.7 oz. chop	0	.63	.18	3.8	n.a.
loin, roasted, lean and fat, 4 oz.	0	1.04	.29	6.4	n.a.
loin, roasted, lean only, 4 oz.	0	1.22	.35	7.4	n.a.
Boston butt, roasted, lean and fat, 4 oz.	0	.57	.26	5.0	n.a.
Boston butt, roasted, lean only, 4 oz.	0	.67	.31	5.9	n.a.
picnic, simmered, lean and fat, 4 oz.	0	.61	.28	5.5	n.a.
picnic, simmered, lean only, 4 oz.	0	.75	.34	6.7	n.a.
spareribs, braised, 4 oz. with bone	0	.49	.24	3.9	n.a.
Pork sausage, see Sausages					
Potato chips, 1 oz.	tr.	.06	.02	1.4	5
Potato sticks, 1 oz.	tr.	.06	.02	1.4	11
Potatoes, white, baked in skin, 1 potato (4¾″ long)	tr.	.15	.07	2.7	31
boiled in skin, 1 round potato (2½″ diam.)	tr.	.12	.05	2.0	22
boiled in skin, diced or sliced, 1 cup	tr.	.14	.06	2.3	25
boiled, pared, 1 round potato (2½″ diam.)	tr.	.12	.05	1.6	22
boiled, pared, diced or sliced, 1 cup	tr.	.14	.05	1.9	25
French-fried, 10 strips (2″–3½″ long)	tr.	.07	.04	1.6	11
fried, 1 cup	tr.	.20	.12	4.8	32
mashed, with milk and butter, 1 cup	360	.17	.11	2.1	19
dry flakes, mashed with water, milk, butter, 1 cup	270	.08	.08	1.9	11
dry granules, mashed with water, milk, butter, 1 cup	230	.08	.11	1.5	6
frozen, French-fried, heated, 10 strips (2″–3½″ long)	tr.	.07	.01	1.3	11

FOOD AND MEASURE	Vit. A (I.U.)	Thia. (mg.)	Rib. (mg.)	Nia. (mg.)	Vit. C (mg.)
frozen, hash brown, cooked, 1 cup	tr.	.11	.03	1.6	12
Potatoes, sweet, baked in skin, 1 potato (5″ long)	9,230	.10	.08	.8	25
boiled in skin, 1 potato (5″ long)	11,940	.14	.09	.9	26
boiled in skin, peeled, mashed, 1 cup	20,150	.23	.15	1.5	43
candied, 1 piece (2½″ long × 2″ diam.)	5,360	.05	.03	.3	9
canned, liquid pack, 4 oz. with liquid	7,145	.07	.05	.5	11
canned, vacuum pack, 4 oz.	8,845	.06	.05	.7	16
canned, vacuum pack, pieces, 1 cup	15,600	.10	.08	1.2	28
Pretzels, all types, 1 oz.	0	.01	.01	.2	0
logs, 10 pretzels (3″ long)	0	.01	.02	.4	0
rods, 1 pretzel (7½″–7¾″ long)	0	tr.	tr.	.1	0
twisted, Dutch, 1 pretzel	0	tr.	tr.	.1	0
twisted, 3-ring, 10 pretzels	0	.01	.01	.2	0
Prickly pear, raw, pulp only, 4 oz.	33	tr.	.01	.2	11
Prune juice, canned, 1 cup	n.a.	.03	.03	1.0	5
Prunes, dehydrated nuggets, 1 cup	2,170	.12	.22	2.1	4
dehydrated nuggets, cooked, sweetened, 1 cup	2,130	.08	.20	2.0	3
dried "softenized," whole, 10 large prunes	1,350	.08	.14	1.4	3
dried, pitted, 10 prunes	1,630	.09	.17	1.6	3
dried, pitted, 1 cup	2,880	.16	.31	2.9	5
dried, pitted, chopped, 1 cup, not packed	2,560	.14	.27	2.6	5
dried, whole, cooked, sweetened, 1 cup	1,430	.06	.14	1.4	2
dried, whole, cooked, unsweetened, 1 cup	1,590	.07	.15	1.5	2
Pudding, mix, starch base, chocolate, cooked, 1 cup	340	.05	.39	.3	2
Pudding, mix, chocolate, instant, prepared, 1 cup	340	.08	.39	.3	2
Pumpkin, fresh, pulp, 4 oz.	1,825	.06	.13	.7	10

Pumpkin, canned, 1 cup	15,680	.07	.12	1.5	12
Pumpkin seed kernels, dry, hulled, 1 cup	100	.34	.27	3.4	n.a.

R

Rabbit, domesticated, stewed, meat only, 4 oz.	n.a.	.06	.08	12.8	n.a.
Radishes, raw, 10 large (1″–1¼″ diam.)	10	.02	.02	.2	21
Radishes, raw, sliced, 1 cup	10	.03	.03	.3	30
Raisins, seedless, whole, 1 cup	30	.16	.12	.7	1
seedless, whole, 1 cup, packed	30	.18	.13	.8	2
seedless, whole, 1 tbsp.	tr.	.01	.01	tr.	tr.
seedless, chopped, 1 cup	30	.15	.11	.7	1
seedless, cooked, sweetened, 1 cup	30	.12	.09	.6	tr.
Raspberries, fresh, black, 1 cup	tr.	.04	.12	1.2	24
fresh, red, 1 cup	160	.04	.11	1.1	31
canned, red, water pack, 1 cup with liquid	220	.02	.10	1.2	22
frozen, red, sweetened, 1 cup	180	.05	.15	1.5	53
Rhubarb, fresh, diced, 1 cup	120	.04	.09	.4	11
cooked, sweetened, 1 cup	220	.05	.14	.8	16
frozen, sweetened, cooked, 1 cup	190	.05	.11	.5	16
Rice, enriched, long grain, brown, cooked, 1 cup	0	.18	.04	2.7	0
white, cooked, 1 cup	0	.23	.02	2.1	0
white, parboiled, cooked, 1 cup	0	.19	.02	2.1	0
white, precooked (instant), fluffed, 1 cup	0	.21	n.a.	1.7	0
Rice polish, stirred, 1 cup	0	1.93	.19	29.6	0
Rockfish, steamed, meat only, 4 oz.	n.a.	.06	.14	n.a.	1
Rolls, commercial, brown-and-serve, baked, 1 oz. roll	tr.	.07	.06	.6	tr.
hard, round or kaiser, 1 roll (3¾″ diam.)	tr.	.13	.12	1.4	tr.
soft, clover leaf, 1 roll (2½″ diam.)	tr.	.08	.05	.6	tr.
soft, frankfurter or hamburger, 1 roll	tr.	.11	.07	.9	tr.
Rutabagas, raw, cubed, 1 cup	810	.10	.10	1.5	60
boiled, drained, cubed or sliced, 1 cup	940	.10	.10	1.4	44
boiled, drained, mashed, 1 cup	1,320	.14	.14	1.9	62

FOOD AND MEASURE	Vit. A (I.U.)	Thia. (mg.)	Rib. (mg.)	Nia. (mg.)	Vit. C (mg.)
Rye flour, dark, 1 cup	0	.78	.28	3.5	0
light, 1 cup	0	.15	.07	.6	0
medium, 1 cup	0	.26	.11	2.2	0

S

FOOD AND MEASURE	Vit. A (I.U.)	Thia. (mg.)	Rib. (mg.)	Nia. (mg.)	Vit. C (mg.)
Salad dressings, commercial, blue cheese, 1 tbsp.	30	tr.	.02	tr.	tr.
Italian, 1 tbsp.	tr.	tr.	tr.	tr.	n.a.
mayonnaise, 1 cup	620	.04	.09	tr.	n.a.
mayonnaise, 1 tbsp.	40	tr.	.01	tr.	n.a.
Roquefort cheese, 1 tbsp.	30	tr.	.02	tr.	tr.
Russian, 1 tbsp.	100	.01	.01	.1	1
salad dressing (mayonnaise type), 1 cup	520	.02	.07	tr.	n.a.
salad dressing (mayonnaise type), 1 tbsp.	30	tr.	tr.	tr.	n.a.
Thousand Islands, 1 tbsp.	50	tr.	tr.	tr.	tr.
Salami, dry, 4 oz.	n.a.	.42	.28	6.1	n.a.
Salami, cooked, 4 oz.	n.a.	.28	.27	4.7	n.a.
Salmon, broiled with butter, meat only, 4 oz.	182	.18	.07	11.2	n.a.
canned, chinook, 1 can with liquid (7¾ oz.)	510	.07	.31	16.1	n.a.
canned, chum, 1 can with liquid (7¾ oz.)	130	.04	.35	15.6	n.a.
canned, coho (silver), 1 can with liquid (7¾ oz.)	180	.07	.40	16.3	n.a.
canned, pink (humpback), 1 can with liquid (7¾ oz.)	150	.07	.40	17.6	n.a.
canned, sockeye (red), 1 can with liquid (7¾ oz.)	510	.09	.35	16.1	n.a.
Salmon roe, raw, 1 oz.	n.a.	.11	.20	.7	5
Salsify, boiled, drained, cubed, 1 cup	10	.04	.05	.3	9
Salt, table, 1 cup	0	0	0	0	0
Sandwich spread, with chopped pickle, 1 tbsp.	40	tr.	tr.	tr.	1
Sardines, Atlantic, canned in oil, 1 can (3¾ oz.)	190	.02	.17	4.7	n.a.
Sardines, Atlantic, canned in oil, drained, 3¼ oz.	200	.03	.18	5.0	n.a.
Sauerkraut, canned in liquid, 1 cup	120	.07	.09	.5	33

Sauerkraut juice, canned, 1 cup	n.a.	.07	.10	.5	44
Sausage, country-style, 4 oz.	n.a.	.25	.22	3.5	n.a.
Polish, 4 oz.	0	.39	.22	3.5	n.a.
pork, 4 oz.	0	.49	.20	2.6	n.a.
pork, canned, 8 oz. can with liquid	0	.43	.43	7.5	n.a.
scrapple, 4 oz.	n.a.	.22	.10	2.1	n.a.
Vienna, canned, drained, 4 oz. (7 sausages)	n.a.	.09	.15	2.9	n.a.
Scallops, bay or sea, raw, meat only, 4 oz.	n.a.	n.a.	.07	1.5	n.a.
Sesame seeds, dry, hulled, 1 tbsp.	n.a.	.01	.01	.4	0
Shad, baked with bacon and butter, 4 oz.	35	.15	.29	9.8	n.a.
Shallots, raw, chopped, 1 tbsp.	tr.	.01	tr.	tr.	1
Sherbet, orange, 1 cup	120	.02	.06	tr.	4
Shrimp, raw, meat only, 4 oz.	n.a.	.02	.03	3.6	n.a.
breaded, fried, 4 oz.	n.a.	.04	.09	3.1	n.a.
canned, drained, 10 large shrimp (3¼″ long)	30	tr.	.02	1.0	n.a.
Snapper, red and grey, raw, meat only, 4 oz.	n.a.	.19	.03	n.a.	n.a.
Soft drinks, carbonated, all flavors, 8 fl. oz.	0	0	0	0	0
Sole, raw, meat only, 4 oz.	n.a.	.06	.06	1.9	n.a.
Soup, canned, condensed, diluted with equal part water or milk:					
asparagus, cream of, with milk, 1 cup	490	.07	.29	.7	tr.
asparagus, cream of, with water, 1 cup	310	.05	.10	.7	n.a.
bean with pork, with water, 1 cup	650	.13	.08	1.0	3
beef broth, boullion or consommé, with water, 1 cup	tr.	tr.	.02	1.2	n.a.
beef noodle, with water, 1 cup	50	.05	.07	1.0	tr.
celery, cream of, with milk, 1 cup	390	.05	.27	.7	2
celery, cream of, with water, 1 cup	190	.02	.05	tr.	tr.
chicken, cream of, with milk, 1 cup	610	.05	.27	.7	2
chicken, cream of, with water, 1 cup	410	.02	.05	.5	tr.
chicken gumbo, with water, 1 cup	220	.02	.05	1.2	5
chicken noodle, with water, 1 cup	50	.02	.02	.7	tr.
chicken with rice, with water, 1 cup	140	tr.	.02	.7	n.a.
chicken vegetable, with water, 1 cup	2,160	.02	.05	1.0	n.a.

FOOD AND MEASURE	Vit. A (I.U.)	Thia. (mg.)	Rib. (mg.)	Nia. (mg.)	Vit. C (mg.)
clam chowder, Manhattan style, with water, 1 cup	880	.02	.02	1.0	n.a.
minestrone, with water, 1 cup	2,350	.07	.05	1.0	n.a.
mushroom, cream of, with milk, 1 cup	250	.05	.34	.7	1
mushroom, cream of, with water, 1 cup	70	.02	.12	.7	tr.
onion, with water, 1 cup	tr.	tr.	.02	tr.	n.a.
pea, green, with milk, 1 cup	530	.10	.28	1.3	10
pea, green, with water, 1 cup	340	.05	.05	1.0	7
pea, split, with water, 1 cup	440	.25	.15	1.5	1
tomato, with milk, 1 cup	1,200	.10	.25	1.3	15
tomato, with water, 1 cup	1,000	.05	.05	1.2	12
turkey noodle, with water, 1 cup	190	.05	.05	1.2	tr.
vegetable beef, with water, 1 cup	2,700	.05	.05	1.0	n.a.
vegetable with beef broth, with water, 1 cup	3,190	.05	.02	1.2	n.a.
vegetarian vegetable, with water, 1 cup	2,940	.05	.05	1.0	n.a.
Soursop, raw, puréed, 1 cup	20	.16	.11	2.0	45
Soy sauce, 1 tbsp.	0	tr.	.05	.1	0
Soybean, mature seeds, dry, raw, 1 cup	170	2.31	.65	4.6	n.a.
Soybean, mature seeds, cooked, 1 cup	50	.38	.16	1.1	0
Soybean, sprouted seeds, see Bean sprouts					
Soybean curd (tofu), 1 piece (2½" × 2¾" × 1")	0	.07	.04	.1	0
Soybean flour, full-fat, 1 cup	90	.72	.26	1.8	0
low-fat, 1 cup	70	.73	.32	2.3	0
defatted, 1 cup	40	1.09	.34	2.6	0
Spaghetti, boiled 8–10 minutes, drained, 1 cup	0	.23	.13	1.8	0
boiled 14–20 minutes, drained, 1 cup	0	.20	.11	1.5	0
canned, in tomato sauce with cheese, 1 cup	930	.35	.28	4.5	10
canned, with meatballs in tomato sauce, 1 cup	1,000	.15	.18	2.3	5
Spinach, raw, chopped, 1 cup	4,460	.06	.11	.3	28
boiled, drained, leaves, 1 cup	14,580	.13	.25	.9	50

canned, 1 cup with liquid	12,760	.05	.23	.7	32
canned, drained, 1 cup	16,400	.04	.25	.6	29
frozen, chopped, boiled, drained, 1 cup	16,200	.14	.31	.8	39
frozen, leaf, boiled, drained, 1 cup	15,390	.15	.27	1.0	53
Squash, summer, scallop, boiled, drained, diced, 1 cup	380	.11	.17	1.7	17
scallop, boiled, drained, sliced, 1 cup	320	.09	.14	1.4	14
yellow, boiled, drained, diced, 1 cup	920	.11	.17	1.7	23
yellow, boiled, drained, sliced, 1 cup	790	.09	.14	1.4	20
zucchini, raw, diced or sliced, 1 cup	420	.07	.12	1.3	25
zucchini, boiled, drained, diced, 1 cup	630	.11	.17	1.7	19
zucchini, boiled, drained, sliced, 1 cup	540	.09	.14	1.4	16
Squash, winter, acorn, baked, ½ squash (4″ diam.)	2,180	.08	.20	1.1	20
acorn, baked, mashed, 1 cup	2,870	.10	.27	1.4	27
acorn, boiled, mashed, 1 cup	2,700	.10	.25	1.0	20
butternut, baked, mashed, 1 cup	13,120	.10	.27	1.4	16
butternut, boiled, mashed, 1 cup	13,230	.10	.25	1.0	12
hubbard, baked, mashed, 1 cup	9,840	.10	.27	1.4	21
hubbard, boiled, diced, 1 cup	9,640	.09	.24	.9	14
hubbard, boiled, mashed, 1 cup	10,050	.10	.25	1.0	15
Strawberries, fresh, whole, 1 cup	90	.04	.10	.9	88
canned, water pack, 1 cup with liquid	100	.02	.07	1.0	48
frozen, sweetened, whole or sliced, 1 cup	80	.05	.15	1.3	135
Succotash, frozen, boiled, drained, 1 cup	510	.15	.09	2.2	10
Sugar, beet or cane, brown, 1 cup firmly packed	0	.02	.07	.4	0
Sugar, beet or cane, granulated or powdered, 1 cup	0	0	0	0	0
Sugar apples (sweetsop), raw, pulp only, 1 cup	30	.25	.35	2.5	85
Sunflower seed kernels, in hull, 1 cup	20	.90	.11	2.5	n.a.
Sunflower seed kernels, hulled, 1 cup	70	2.84	.33	7.8	n.a.
Sweetbreads, calf, braised, 3 oz.	n.a.	.05	.14	2.5	n.a.

FOOD AND MEASURE	Vit. A (I.U.)	Thia. (mg.)	Rib. (mg.)	Nia. (mg.)	Vit. C (mg.)
Sweet potatoes, see Potatoes, sweet					
Swordfish, raw, meat only, 4 oz.	1,800	.06	.06	9.1	n.a.
Swordfish, broiled with butter,					
meat only, 4 oz.	2,185	.04	.05	11.4	n.a.
Syrup, chocolate, fudge type, 1 tbsp.	30	.01	.04	.1	tr.
chocolate, thin type, 1 tbsp.	tr.	tr.	.02	.1	0
molasses, blackstrap, 1 tbsp.	n.a.	.02	.04	.4	n.a.
table, corn or corn and maple,					
1 tbsp.	0	0	0	0	0

T

FOOD AND MEASURE	Vit. A (I.U.)	Thia. (mg.)	Rib. (mg.)	Nia. (mg.)	Vit. C (mg.)
Tangerine, fresh, 1 large (2½" diam.)	420	.06	.02	.1	31
Tangerine, fresh, sections, 1 cup	820	.12	.04	.2	60
Tangerine juice, fresh, 1 cup	1,040	.15	.05	.2	77
canned, 1 cup	1,040	.15	.05	.2	54
frozen, diluted, 1 cup	1,020	.14	.04	.3	67
Tapioca, dry, 1 tbsp.	0	0	0	0	0
Tartare sauce, commercial, 1 cup	510	.02	.07	tr.	2
Tartare sauce, commercial, 1 tbsp.	30	tr.	tr.	tr.	tr.
Tomato, green, raw, 1 lb.	1,110	.25	.17	2.1	83
Tomato, ripe, raw, 1 tomato					
(2⅖" diam.; 3½ oz.)	820	.05	.04	.6	21
raw, 1 tomato (3" diam.; 7 oz.)	1,640	.11	.07	1.3	42
boiled, drained, 1 cup	2,410	.17	.12	1.9	58
canned, 1 cup with liquid	2,170	.12	.07	1.7	41
Tomato juice, canned, 1 cup	1,940	.12	.07	1.9	39
Tomato juice cocktail, canned,					
1 cup	1,940	.12	.05	1.5	39
Tomato paste, canned, 6-oz. can	5,610	.34	.20	5.3	83
Tomato purée, canned, 4 oz.	1,815	.10	.06	1.6	38
Tongue, beef, medium-fat,					
braised, 4 oz.	n.a.	.06	.33	4.0	n.a.
Tuna, canned in oil, 7-oz. can	180	.08	.18	20.0	n.a.
canned in oil, drained, 1 cup	130	.08	.19	19.0	n.a.
canned in water, 7-oz. can	n.a.	n.a.	.20	26.3	n.a.
Turkey, roasted, dark meat only,					
4 oz.	n.a.	.05	.26	4.8	n.a.
dark meat only, diced, 1 cup	n.a.	.06	.32	5.9	n.a.
light meat only, 4 oz.	n.a.	.06	.16	12.6	n.a.
light meat only, diced, 1 cup	n.a.	.07	.20	15.5	n.a.
canned, meat only, 1 cup	270	.04	.29	9.6	n.a.

Turkey, potted, 1 cup	n.a.	.07	.50	2.7	n.a.
Turkey pot pie, frozen, 8 oz.	3,015	.25	.30	5.7	5
Turnip greens, raw, trimmed, 1 lb.	34,470	.95	1.77	3.6	631
boiled in small amount water, drained, 1 cup	9,140	.22	.35	.9	100
boiled in large amount water, drained, 1 cup	8,270	.15	.33	.7	68
canned, 1 cup with liquid	10,900	.05	.21	1.4	44
frozen, chopped, boiled, drained, 1 cup	11,390	.08	.15	.7	31
Turnips, raw, cubed or sliced, 1 cup	tr.	.05	.09	.8	47
boiled, drained, cubed, 1 cup	tr.	.06	.08	.5	34
boiled, drained, mashed, 1 cup	tr.	.09	.12	.7	51

V

Veal, chuck, stewed, meat only, 4 oz.	n.a.	.10	.33	7.2	n.a.
chuck, stewed, meat only, diced, 1 cup	n.a.	.13	.41	9.0	n.a.
loin chop, broiled, meat only, 4 oz.	n.a.	.08	.28	6.1	n.a.
loin, broiled, meat only, diced, 1 cup	n.a.	.10	.35	7.6	n.a.
rib, roasted, meat only, 4 oz.	n.a.	.15	.35	8.9	n.a.
rib, roasted, meat only, diced, 1 cup	n.a.	.18	.43	10.9	n.a.
round, rump (leg cutlet), broiled, meat only, 4 oz.	n.a.	.08	.28	6.1	n.a.
Vegetable juice cocktail, canned, 1 cup	1,690	.12	.07	1.9	22
Vegetables, see individual listings					
Vegetables, mixed, frozen, boiled, drained, 1 cup	9,010	.22	.13	2.0	15
Venison, raw, meat only, 4 oz.	n.a.	.05	.10	1.4	n.a.

W-Y-Z

Waffle, mix, baked, 1 round waffle (7″ diam.)	170	.11	.17	.7	tr.
Waffle, mix, baked, 1 square waffle (9″ diam.)	460	.28	.46	1.8	1
Walnuts, black, in shell, 1 lb.	300	.22	.11	.7	n.a.
black, shelled, 1 cup	1,360	1.00	.50	3.2	n.a.
black, shelled, chopped, 1 tbsp.	20	.02	.01	.1	n.a.
English, in shell, 1 lb.	60	.67	.27	1.8	4
English, shelled, 1 lb.	140	1.50	.59	4.1	9
English, shelled, halves, 1 cup	30	.33	.13	.9	2
English, shelled, chopped, 1 tbsp.	tr.	.03	.01	.1	tr.

FOOD AND MEASURE	Vit. A (I.U.)	Thia. (mg.)	Rib. (mg.)	Nia. (mg.)	Vit. C (mg.)
Water chestnuts, raw, 4 oz.	0	.12	.18	.9	4
Watercress, leaves and stems, raw, whole, 1 cup	1,720	.03	.06	.3	28
Watercress, leaves and stems, finely chopped, 1 cup	6,130	.10	.20	1.1	99
Watermelon, 1 wedge with rind (10″ diam. × 1″ thick)	2,510	.13	.13	.9	30
Watermelon, diced pieces, 1 cup	940	.05	.05	.3	11
Weakfish, broiled with butter, meat only, 4 oz.	n.a.	.11	.09	4.0	n.a.
Wheat flour, whole wheat, stirred, 1 cup	0	.66	.14	5.2	0
white, all-purpose, sifted, 1 cup	0	.51	.30	4.0	0
white, all-purpose, unsifted, 1 cup	0	.55	.33	4.4	0
white, bread, sifted, 1 cup	0	.51	.30	4.0	0
white, bread, unsifted, 1 cup	0	.60	.36	4.8	0
white, cake or pastry, sifted, 1 cup	0	.03	.03	.7	0
white, cake or pastry, unsifted, 1 cup	0	.04	.04	.8	0
white, self-rising, sifted, 1 cup	0	.51	.30	4.0	0
white, self-rising, unsifted, 1 cup	0	.55	.33	4.4	0
Wheat germ, cereal, see Cereals					
Wheat, parboiled, see Bulgur					
Whey, fluid, 1 cup	20	.07	.34	.2	n.a.
Whitefish, lake, raw, meat only, 4 oz.	2,565	.16	.14	3.4	n.a.
White sauce, medium, 1 cup	1,150	.10	.43	.5	2
Wild rice, raw, 1 cup	0	.72	1.01	9.9	0
Wine, dessert, 18.8% alcohol, 3½ fl. oz. glass	n.a.	.01	.02	.2	n.a.
Wine, table, 12.2% alcohol, 3½ fl. oz. glass	n.a.	tr.	.01	.1	n.a.
Yam, tuber, raw, 4 oz.	tr.	.10	.04	.5	9
Yeast, baker's, compressed, 1 cake (1¼″ square)	tr.	.13	.30	2.0	tr.
Yeast, baker's, dry, active, 1 package (¼ oz.)	tr.	.16	.38	2.6	tr.
Yogurt, from partially skim milk, 8-oz. container	150	.09	.41	.2	2
Yogurt, from whole milk, 8-oz. container	320	.07	.36	.2	2
Zucchini, see Squash, summer					